GATHER AT THE RIVER

Twenty-Five Authors on Fishing

GATHER at THE RIVER

25 Authors on Fishing

Edited by

DAVID JOY
with **ERIC RICKSTAD**

HUB CITY PRESS
SPARTANBURG, SC

BOOK DESIGN: Meg Reid
COVER ILLUSTRATION: by Basecamp Printing in Charleston, WV
INTERIOR ILLUSTRATIONS: by Jaclyn Reyes
PROOFREADER: Jacquelyn Lancaster

Ron Rash's essay, "Fishing Lessons," was originally published in *Garden & Gun* (August/September 2013).

Parts of J. Drew Lanham's essay, "Dream Fishing," appeared in the book *The Home Place* by J. Drew Lanham, published by Milkweed Editions, 2017.

Jill McCorkle's essay, "The Mullet Girls," was originally published by *The Washington Post* (July 30, 2000).

Natalie Baszile's essay, "Frogging Quintana," was originally published in *The Best Women's Travel Writing, Vol. 9* published by Travelers' Tale, 2013.

Library of Congress Cataloging-in-Publication Data

Names: Joy, David, 1983- editor. | Rickstad, Eric, editor.
Title: Gather at the river : twenty-five authors on fishing / edited by David Joy and Eric Rickstad.
Description: [Spartanburg, South Carolina] : Hub City Press, [2019]
Identifiers: LCCN 2018031214| ISBN 9781938235528 (book) | ISBN 9781938235535 (eBook)
Subjects: LCSH: Fishing—Literary collections.
Classification: LCC PN6071.F47 G38 2019 | DDC 808.83/9579—dc23
LC record available at https://lccn.loc.gov/2018031214

Underwriting for Jaclyn Reyes illustrations provided by Katherine Wakefield

HUB CITY
PRESS

186 W. Main Street
Spartanburg, SC 29306
864.577.9349
www.hubcity.org

Because there is a kind of faith with fishing. It is the belief that the brevity of all things is not bitter, but a calm moment beside calm water is enough to still the breaking of all hearts everywhere.

—Alex Taylor, from "The Evening Part of the Daylight"

TABLE OF CONTENTS

Introduction
DAVID JOY

I was lucky in that I grew up in a family of fishermen. All my life I had people who took me to water. There's a picture of me maybe four years old with a mess of catfish bending me sideways. I'm standing in the driveway at the house where I grew up in Charlotte, North Carolina. I have the weight of the fish balanced on my shoulder, and the channel cats run the stringer from my head to my feet.

Since the beginning, fishing has been at the heart of everything I am.

When I was a kid, my family went to the Outer Banks each fall. They'd time the trip for late October or early November, try to catch the runs of redfish and seatrout as the fish pour out of inlets and turn south. I was eleven years old when I finally got to go.

My grandmother had given me my first saltwater rod that Christmas. Growing up in a family of outdoorsmen, there are moments that mark significant points along the journey—your first pocketknife, the first time you're handed a rifle. The rod she gave me still stands out as the best present I ever got. When I think about why, it's because it seemed to mark a sort of acceptance. I wasn't just some tag-along kid anymore. I was one of them.

That fall I missed a week of sixth grade for the trip. Even after all these years I remember how cold my hands were as I scaled fish under the rental house, everyone in the family doing a job, all of us smiling and laughing as we cleaned the day's catch. I can remember the way the playing cards smelled as someone shuffled the deck, a running game of Rummy continuing each night. But more than anything, it's an image. It's a late afternoon on the Atlantic with the sun fading, me watching my grandmother catch a fish.

A cold November wind blew in from the east, shifting sand and pushing the smell of seawater inland. Past the breakers, where the ocean flattened into one continuous line, the sky blended from cobalt to orange along the horizon; higher, flax yellow gradually rising to white. The winter sun dropped behind sprigs of sea oats, slowly sinking into the dunes. A slick pane of wetted sand shone like a sheet of glass.

My family stood along the shore, each member angling a line into sea green breakers. Their darkened silhouettes grew smaller down the beach, each shadow holding a rod that bowed to incoming tide. The profile farthest away turned hard toward the dunes and the rod doubled over. My grandmother had a fish.

Everyone along the shore turned and looked at her for a second before concentrating again on the pull of his or her own rod. I stared at my family stretched down the cold shoreline, my grandmother reeling in a spot, the first stars coming into view over the ocean. These are the types of details that have always stayed with me. Times in the woods and on water.

All I know of beauty I learned with a fishing rod in my hand.

That fact lies at the heart of why this book exists. Every writer in these pages believes there is no substitute for what can be learned by time on the water. Collectively we wanted this book to benefit the C.A.S.T. For Kids Foundation, a fishing-related nonprofit that operates three programs: C.A.S.T. for Kids, Fishing Kids, and Take A Warrior Fishing. C.A.S.T. for Kids focuses on special-needs children and their caretakers, Fishing Kids on urban youth, while Take A Warrior Fishing supports military personnel and their families, all three programs working to get people, and especially children, on the water.

The truth is I can't imagine having grown up without a river. There were years where I didn't miss a day on the water. Literally, not a day. Nowadays, I don't get out quite as often as I used to, but I still fish fifty or sixty days a year. I make my living as a novelist and that allows me to be in the woods more than most. Another benefit is that I've gotten to know some of the most talented writers at work today, and I'm lucky enough to call them friends. This book is a culmination of those two things—my obsession with fishing and the kindness of incredibly talented friends.

In this book, twenty-five award-winning and bestselling authors were asked simply to write about fishing. Some, like *New York Times* bestselling author Eric Rickstad, who helped me edit, are just as passionate about the sport as I am. Others like Erik Storey self-admittedly can't flip a button cast. But *Gather at the River* isn't a collection of big fish stories. The tales here aren't even centered on rod and reel. There are essays about digging worms, running lobster traps, and feeling like bait when you're swimming with sharks. This is PEN/Faulkner Finalist Ron

Rash writing about the mountains of his youth. It's C.J. Box explaining where he wants his ashes spread when he dies. This is an anthology about friendship, family, love and loss, and everything in between.

With stories ranging from Puerto Rico to Australia, from chasing trout in Appalachian streams to grabbing frogs in a Louisiana swamp, these pages are filled with laughter and tears. There is grit, there is beauty, and there is the overwhelming power of memory, because as Thoreau wrote, "Many men go fishing all of their lives without knowing that it is not really the fish they are after." This book is a diverse testament to that fact. But above all else, this book will get a few kids on the water who might not otherwise have the chance. So for that, dear reader, thank you.

We hope you enjoy the stories.

Gould's Inlet
TAYLOR BROWN

We rolled up to the beach in a battered Jeep Cherokee, the sandy pavement crackling beneath our tires. My friend Lee Hopkins threw the shifter into park. He was an ace shortstop and near-scratch golfer with summer-blond hair and freckles. Hints of pink showed underneath his clear eyes, like ballplayer's eye paint. His true love was marshes and streams.

Before us lay Gould's Inlet, the narrow entrance to the river and salt marsh that divided the island we lived on—Saint Simons Island in southeast Georgia—from the southern point of Sea Island, an exclusive resort where I worked at the bicycle shop, renting beach cruisers to well-heeled vacationers. We were sixteen years old.

The inlet glittered like a long sword under the summer sun, slicing through the soft flesh of beaches and sandbars. A beautiful streak of water, but deadly. The tide roared through here as through a sluice. Old signs, thick with bird droppings, warned against swimming.

Strong athletes, with white teeth and golden arms, had disappeared here. Once, the inlet sucked a pair of doctors out to sea. They spent a whole night in open water, their eyes swollen shut from the salt. They removed their trousers and tied off the legs, like we learned in Boy Scouts, making improvised life vests. Blinded, they didn't know they were safe until the incoming tide thrust them back on the beach.

Low tide had revealed the vast sandbar jutting more than a mile out from the beach. The very tip of this peninsula verged on deep water— our destination. We lifted the rear gate of the Jeep and chose our rods for the day from the quiver running the length of the interior. We took a five-gallon bucket full of tackle and a red Igloo cooler. The latter was faded the color of an old brick, loaded with ice and bait, bottled water and Coca-Cola.

My father spent much of his childhood on the water in Saint Petersburg, Florida. Skiing, fishing, boating. However, we would not own a boat until later in high school, when one of his friends gave us a hard-worn old ski boat he couldn't sell. So, the fishing of my youth was mainly this: surf fishing.

We crossed a boardwalk to a strip of soft sand that crunched like snow under our feet. Here, beachgoers lay on their towels, oil-glazed under the sun, their bodies baking like Krispy Kreme donuts. We descended these postcard sands and crossed a wide stream, ankle-deep, at the foot of the beach. This was a minor branch of Gould's Inlet, dividing the upper beach from the vast expanse of the sandbar.

On the far side of the stream, the sand became immediately darker, harder, rippled by hydraulic action. The ground was strangely cool beneath our feet, as if we were walking on the bottom of the sea. At any time but low tide, we would be.

We walked and walked across this vast desert of sand—wave-ridged, hard as stone, like the surface of an alien world. We splashed through tidal pools, piss-warm, where tiny schools of baitfish shot back and forth in their formations, trapped by the outgoing tide. Gulls wheeled and screamed overhead, trailing us like a shrimp boat. From a distance, we must have looked like bizarre pilgrims, burdened with our jangling array of rods and nets and tackle. Our boonie hats squirmed and flopped in the breeze, trying to lift from our heads.

My feet hurt, hurt, hurt. I was born with clubfeet, my ankles twisted so that my soles met like praying hands. Straightening them had necessitated a slew of reconstructive surgeries—the most recent just three months before, right after school got out. My summer, so far, had been morphine drips and bedpans, sponge baths and paperbacks and balsa-wood model airplanes. A month ago, I had watched my doctor remove a six-inch pin from the heel of my left foot with a pair of vice-grip pliers.

The sand here, hammered into such stony ridges, throbbed through my soles. I focused into the distance, the creamy roll of the breakers, where the sandbar dropped like a shelf into deeper water. The sea looked nearly black beyond the surf, flecked with silver shards of sun.

When I think of the water of the Georgia coast—my home—I think of shadow and murk. Mystery. Four blackwater rivers empty their mouths along the seaward edge of the state, including the "Amazon of the South," the Altamaha. That mighty river, undammed, is storied for torpedo-size sturgeon and alligator gar—armored fish which slink through the lightless currents like prehistoric relics. Then there's the famed sea monster of the coast, the Altamaha-ha, which haunts my second novel, *The River of Kings*.

The Altamaha delivered the alluvium that built these barrier islands, raising them over eons from the sea. The same dark sediment muddies the water here, so that the palm of your hand, spread pale and flat beneath the waves, will disappear just six inches beneath the surface. In the shallows, you never know where your next step will fall. Such water breeds mystery, legend. Fear.

We kept trudging across the expanse, reaching the foamy slurp of the waterline. Soon we were cradled in the surf, belly-deep, casting our lines. White shreds of bait—squid—flew like tiny ghosts from our poles, twisting and fluttering through the air. They landed beyond the shelf of the bar. They sank into the darkness, their pale flesh hiding the stainless gleam of hooks.

Green mountain chains of surf rose before us, again and again, only to tumble and crash in our wake, lathering the sands in foam. Soon my pain began to dissipate. I was lightened. I rode the swells with my hips, bouncing from the bottom in slow motion. I had the strange buoyancy of an astronaut.

In reality, I didn't care much about catching fish. For me, on the walk out, this outing had ceased to be about fishing or adventure or even friendship. It had become a test. The same as most any outdoor concert or school dance or Boy Scout hike—anything that required me to stand or walk for longer than an hour. I didn't care about the fish, like I didn't care about the band or the football game or the destination of the trail. I cared about getting it done, the same as everyone else.

Lee was different. He had come with ambition. He was here to catch fish. He squinted over the breakers, his face freckled and sun-pinked. He had the easy grace of the gifted athlete, which I envied. He seemed born to wield baseball bats and golf clubs and fishing rods. I had watched him knock the red clay from his cleats and lift his Easton Black Magic bat swirling over his shoulder and rope the first pitch straight over the centerfield fence. Meanwhile, I was stuck in right field, last on the batting order.

I envied Lee, but I respected him. We used to play one-on-one tackle football in his front yard, with his father for all-time quarterback. I remember Lee catching an accidental forearm shiver while going for a sack. We were maybe ten. Lee rose grinning, licking the blood from his mouth. You can only love a kid like that.

Still, he wasn't accustomed to striking out, even if he was up against the ocean. He was getting frustrated. His eyes had turned to firing slits. The muscles flickered in his temples and cheeks. Meanwhile, the sun was beginning to slip, falling slanted at our backs. Soon the tide would rise, slipping over this vast peninsula of sand. It already was. We'd moved our tackle farther up the beach, twice.

Lee reeled in his line. The twin hooks were naked, like steely question marks.

"What you think?" I asked.

Lee's gaze remained fixed on the surf, the dark valley beyond the breakers.

"Ten more minutes," he said, rebaiting his hooks.

I shrugged. "Sure."

Ten minutes. Fifteen. I felt the tide crawling higher up my belly, but I wasn't worried. The sun had lulled me, the roll of surf. I was not in pain. Still, I was about ready to go. I wanted to get started on the hike back to the car—to get past it.

Twenty minutes. Lee reeled in his line, his teeth gritted. Defeat in his face. I was looking at him, hoping he was ready to leave, when the black antenna of my rod snapped double, nearly yanked from hands.

"I got something, Lee! I got something!"

Lee's eyes jumped open. He came wading and splashing toward me, holding his rod over the water.

"Big mother!" I told him.

I could feel the strength of the creature through the line. A whip of muscle, cracking with power. The fury of a hooked jaw was wired right into my palms, zero distortion. The fish was talking to me, saying *I am deep and mad and strong*. The message was wordless and pure.

A swell broke around my chest, that high, and I knew—quick as the stab of a knife—that I was out of my element, trapped in alien country. You were not supposed to get scared fishing, I thought. Not supposed to go squid-soft and pale.

Lee looked at the tortured graphite, the singing line. I looked at him.

"What should I do?"

"Let him run," said Lee. "Whenever he lets up, tighten the drag and reel like a sonofabitch."

"He ain't letting up. He's a whale, Lee."

"Whales ain't got teeth, son."

Whatever this fish was, it was unbelievably strong. I pictured a big stingray, shooting along the bottom like a stealth bomber, trailing that spiked whip of tail. Or something else. I thought of the yellowy Polaroids tacked up in a nearby bait shop, showing the bloody red mouths of sharks caught off the municipal pier. People said that Saint Simons Sound—the strait between here and Jekyll Island, one mile south—was the largest shark breeding ground on the east coast.

The fish streaked laterally across the horizon, pulling the line danger-ously taut. Swells were rolling against my chest. I could reel only in jerks. I started staggering backward, backpedaling, dragging the fish toward shallower water. I was soft from the surgery, out of shape. The tendons of my arms burned like lit fuses. My breath was fast and hoarse, my saliva thick enough to chew. I could feel my heart in my ears, throbbing. Lee kept shouting instructions.

"I'm trying, goddammit!"

The tug-of-war continued. Five yards, ten. Fifteen. Then a long wave rose before us, rolling high and green into the sun. The line skittered up through the rising water, and there, silhouetted inside the sunshot greenhouse of the swell, was the fish I'd hooked.

"Shark!"

The silhouette was unmistakable: sharp as the point of a spear, finned like a jet fighter. Fear broke through my blood. I could feel my own kidneys dangling in the red sea of my blood. My newly-sutured foot felt small and twisted, my wasted calf glowing like a fish belly in the dark water, just asking for teeth. I'd heard of sharks attacking beachgoers in waist-deep surf.

Still, I didn't think to cut the line. It was not courage or fear or pride. It simply didn't occur to me, as if I'd been hooked myself—a stainless barb in my own jaw or hands or heart. I could feel every twitch and throttle of the creature through the thin white sinew of the line. I could picture him whipping through the darkness, trailing a red string of blood from his mouth.

I kept staggering backward in the surf, heaving the rod like a giant lever. I could hardly get enough air. My arms no longer burned. They felt willowy and strange, spent. But it was working. The surf crashed and foamed around our waists. Then our thighs, our knees. We were rising taller from the water, step after step. Retreating toward dry land. Supremacy.

When my heel struck the exposed sand of the bar, I dug into a crouch, straining against the line. The fish had tired, but it seemed made of pure lead or iron now, like I was hauling in an anchor. I reeled and heaved, reeled and heaved. At the height of my pull, just when my tendons seemed ready to break, the line went sudden-soft, spiraling into a long curly-cue. At the other end, a panicked splashing in the surf. Lee jumped in place, sighting over the foam.

"He's grounded!"

We approached on our tiptoes, the tide swirling around our ankles. The shark was beached in two inches of water. He flopped weakly, near-dead from the fight. He wasn't as big as I thought—possibly four feet long. His iron-gray fuselage gleamed in the sun. His fins carried dark points, as if dipped in ink.

"Blacktip," said Lee.

The fish lay flat on his belly, gills flared. Asphyxiating. The hook hung from a ragged cavity of mouth flesh. The black fins flailed like undergrown wings. The eyes were buttonlike, wide. This deadly creature, which I had torn from the surf, was dying at my feet.

Guilt stabbed through my chest, sucking out my breath. I felt a sudden panic. Lee was squatting beside the fish, twisting the hook free with a pair of needle-nose pliers. Without thinking, I dropped to one knee and scooped my hands under the fish's belly. Lee raised the freed hook like a question.

"The hell?"

Before he could stop me, I'd hefted the fish high from the beach and gone running back into the surf. I ran high-kneed, holding the fish at arm's length, belly-up, like some offering to the sea kings. Neptune or Poseidon. Lee had told me about *tonic immobility*—the hypnotic state that sharks and rays entered when inverted. In the Farallon Islands, off San Francisco, killer whales were known to hold great white sharks upside down, killing them.

It didn't work. The shark exploded to life in my hands, whipping and thrashing with astonishing violence, his teeth flashing bright. I could hardly hold him. I was hardly knee-deep in the surf when I heaved the shark from my hands like a bomb. I remember the fish whirling toward me in midair, flashing his wicked grin, but I was already wheeling in the opposite direction. I ran for my damn life, imagining those selfsame teeth snapping my Achilles tendons like rubber bands.

Back on the beach, I collapsed with dramatic effect. Lee squatted over me.

"That, boy, was probably the *dumbest shit* I have ever seen."

When I got up, I saw that the tide had crept high up the bar, swirling and foaming around our tackle. Likely, it would have reached the shark in time. Likely. As for us, we now faced a mile-long hike to shore, the surf eating up the sandbar in our wake.

We gathered up our gear and started across the sand. We marched toward the afternoon sun, trailing long tails of shadow. I thought I could feel the steel staples in my foot, aching in the bone. The mouth-shaped wound in my heel, where they pulled out the steel pin, howled. But the pain was different now. A choice I had made. I could limp with pride.

Then we reached the tidal cut. The stream, ankle-deep on the hike out, had swelled with the incoming tide. It was as wide as a small river now, dark with depth. Who knew how deep. The surface was wind-riffled, sliding between the banks like the scaled skin of a snake. That fast.

I looked at Lee.

"You think we can cross okay?"

Lee looked back at the crashing line of surf, so much closer now.

"I don't think we have a choice."

He hefted the five-gallon bucket of tackle onto his head and stepped into the shallows.

"Wade with your feet wide," he said. "Straddle-legged."

I nodded, followed. The current tugged at our ankles, our calves, our knees. The tide seemed to have fingers. They curled around our legs, drawing us toward the sucking mouth of the inlet. We waded deeper, deeper, descending toward the middle of the stream.

When the water reached our waists, I started thinking about sharks again. We grew up knowing they were around, but I could *feel* their proximity now, as if I were still wired to that blacktip. Sharks were no longer abstractions. They were throbbing through the darkness, fierce and strong. They were *here*. I sensed my power sinking with every step, every inch of depth. In two feet of water, I was a king. In four feet, meat.

At midstream, the tide reached our chests. We held our gear over our heads. The current bumped and eddied at our throats, threatening to topple us. We could be sucked out into the deep black water of the inlet, drowned, or my blacktip shark could come for revenge, tearing into our bellies or underparts. Or both. The water brushed my chin.

Then we were rising again, climbing the far bank, the bottom ridged beneath us like steps. We emerged onto the soft sand of the upper beach, man-tall, breathing hard. The sunbathers were all but gone, fled from the lengthening shadows. We made for the boardwalk, the sand squeaking beneath our feet.

Soon we were standing at the Jeep, looking back at the sandbar. It was nearly gone, a spit of sand at the mouth of the inlet. An island barely escaped. The tide was moving fast like a river, flooding the place. I thought of the living weapon we had pulled from the dark country of that water, then put back.

That day, we were kings.

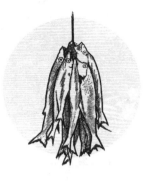

Lullaby

J.C. SASSER

f I die before you wake, there is something I must tell you. As your mother, I must.

Like you, little men, I was a child once. We lived in a house, but we grew up in the South Georgia woods, acres and acres of it. It's where I smoked my first pine straw, stepped on my first nail, and examined my first *Playboy*. It's the place that made me wild.

Behind our old house is a dirt road. You know the one. It's a mile long and cuts through endless games of hide-and-go-seek and tall green soldiers of pine. The dogwoods you see lining the road were planted over half a century ago by Mema and Granny Sills. She's Mema to me, great-grandma Rubye to you. She was born with a veil over her face. The midwife said it was a sign of supernatural power. Mema could make warts disappear with a penny and a piece of Scotch tape and her magic touch kept a thousand dogwood seedlings alive through a terrible drought. Her trees are still there, and their offspring run wild all over the woods like little miracles. Mema had vision, gave up a dream house to buy this land.

I've been carried down this road. I've crawled down this road, walked it and run it. I've barefooted it and punched its spine with stiletto heels. I've tricycled it, bicycled it, and ridden it bareback on a jackass named Hokey. I've Honda 50'd it, Yamaha 80'd it, Kawasaki 250'd it, and my brother, Hec, and I have scarred it with fishtails, pretending we were Bo and Luke Duke and that Mama's bombed-out Chrysler was The General Lee.

Not much has changed about this road. You'll still see tortoises and wild hare, swallowtails, and great spangled fritillaries. You'll still see fox and flying squirrels, turkeys, and coveys of quail. Although they're here, you won't see deer on the road. They're smarter than most deer, a result of the pressure my Daddy put on them for years and whose memory is whispered to their young, knowing it helps keep them alive.

The only thing that's different is there's no field at the curve. The gas tank for Carlton's tractor is gone. And so is he. He and his wife, Claudine, gone in an instant.

At the end of the road is the clubhouse. It's exclusive in every sense of the word, and you're lucky you're part of the club. It's an old World War II barracks, modified with a front porch with cypress tree pillars and cypress tree rails you can't trust. There are no lace curtains or lightning rods, and the only reason it has a bathroom is because in 1955 somebody invited the governor. He needed some rest and relaxation and, apparently, a respectable place to piss.

Some of it has changed since I was a child. The floor is spongier and slopes a little more. Some of the things in it are mine now. Daddy's deer and arrowheads, the rattlesnake skin, the saber-tooth cat mount, and the whale vertebra pierced with a megalodon's tooth. There's an additional bathroom now and a special place where you can bunk. The towels are arranged by color in the drawer, and the hallway is decorated with photographs of all your kin. That's your Gaga's touch. It belongs to her now. She, too, has vision. You'll still find rats in the traps, maybe a snake, but you won't find a cup of worms in the fridge or a box of crickets chirping on the screened-in porch.

Down the hill from the clubhouse is the pond, twenty-five acres of wet black mirror. The water smells the same way it's always smelled, a smell I can't bottle, like childhood. The cypress in front of the dock has rotted, but its stump is still there decorated with somebody's fishing line and faded red floater. The sand Mema hauled in once lightened the bank. It's where we built sand castles and let minnows nibble our toes. Grass now grows in that little spot, but in the shallows, you can still see minnows and evidence of that stark white sand.

This is Reedy Creek. We call it Reedy for short. Mema named it that because the creek that feeds the pond is reedy. It's a place we come to escape. It's a place we come to fish. It's a place we come to gather.

I don't remember catching my first fish. Nobody does. Like you, little man, I was the second child. But everybody remembers Hec's. He was three. He pulled in a bluegill off the dock, took one look at it fighting on the line, and said, "Damn."

I've caught my fair share of fish. Red and yellow breasts, catfish, bluegills, and bass, and I've caught my fair share of weeds, logs, beer cans, and sunglasses manufactured in the fifties.

I've used all kinds of bait. Red wrigglers, nightcrawlers, and spitballs of Sunbeam White. I've lured my line with Beetle Spins, glitter worms, and crickets, of which I went through a spell of sampling myself.

"You better stop eating those crickets. They'll snatch out your voice and you won't be able to talk," Mema told me as I snuck one head-first in my mouth. That was the end of that.

I've fished with cane poles, rods and reels, sticks, buckets, and my pinkie toe when I had nothing else.

But what I remember most about fishing was what happened after the fish were caught, on the screened-in porch with the drainboard sink and the two wooden tables that stretch twenty feet long. After sunset, they'd bring in the stringers, garlands upon garlands of kaleidoscopic fish. They'd bring in the Styrofoam and red Igloo coolers full of flopping loot. The men would come in and have a seat, and the women who had outfished them would come out with knives. Twilight would set in.

You'd hear the faucet squeak on and the water spew from the pipe. You'd hear scraping, scratching, ripping flesh, and cracking bone. You'd hear guts slop in a bucket. And if you listened close enough, you'd hear blood, little rivers of it running. Mama'd be there, barefooted in cut-off shorts with her long, love-at-first-sight legs, tearing off a head. Pam would be there with her viper-eyes, sweet-talking and flinging scales into her flaming red hair. Wanda would crack a joke with bream eggs in her hand, and Mema, more glamorous than a young Liz Taylor, would be there laughing with fish guts on her diamonds. A moth might flutter by, a whippoorwill might scream. And I'd be under their feet, wondering how could so much murder be so pretty?

Somebody would light the fryer. You'd smell hot grease. I'd run over to watch Mama drop in a fish, and I'd stare into a swirling black galaxy of cornmeal shooting stars, tempted in a weird way to put my fingers in it.

J.T. always said the blessing, before him it was Hines. It got to Harold after J.T. died and now it's Bond's job. One day I hope it will be one of yours. We would sit and eat what we had worked for, what we had caught. After supper, I'd slide underneath the table and hide among cords of naked knees. In a few minutes, they'd get to telling stories.

They told stories of the people who died before I was born and never got to meet. Like my snuff chewing great grandmother, Vida, how she fished from the banks and was never seen in a boat, how you could hear her squealing all the way up the hill every time she hooked a redeye, how if the bream weren't biting it was the signs, and if they were, she'd hike her dress up and go out deeper.

They told stories about Jew Baby, a man who served time for cracking safes and worked off his sentence in the Georgia State pen, cleaning debris from the electric chair helmets. Jew Baby had a stutter and a fat wife named Maw-rie. He'd come out to Reedy with a pole, a croaker sack, and a can of gasoline to catch rattlesnakes for the Rattlesnake Roundup. After he competed and collected his prize money, he'd kill the snakes, eat or freeze the meat and make wallets and belts out of their hide.

I never knew Jew Baby, but my ass certainly did. It's been striped many a time by a belt he made for my Daddy. You know the belt. We call it The Rattlesnake Belt.

The first time you felt its venom I'd caught you trying to hide the matchbox cars you'd stolen out of the classroom's toy bin your first day of pre-school. Stealing, little men, deserves a whipping in my book.

"Why're you being so mean to your little brother?" I asked you a few days later.

"That rattlesnake's still in me," you said.

And I smiled, proud at knowing Jew Baby lives in you, too.

They'd tell stories about Marshall A. Byrd, also known as Model-A. Fresh out of Reidsville prison, Model-A walked into great uncle Hines's furniture store and asked for a job. When Hines asked Model-A if he'd killed a man, Model-A said, "No sir. I didn't kill him. I just cut him. And he died."

They'd tell about old times, about the Depression and the Tinker

Man. About my great granddaddy, Sheriff Tom Watson Brantley, who never learned to drive. They'd tell that sad story of how one of his prisoners who he thought he'd redeemed shot his heart out. After that, things would get quiet for a while until somebody else told another story. They'd tell stories about Aunt Soph and Saphie Sarina Sapphire. They'd tell stories about the good times, the summers out here, playing bridge, and couples taking turns by the woodpile. They'd tell about that one time they left the children on the hill, caught ninety-eight fish, and returned to find little Wanda had almost chopped off her foot with an axe. It's a miracle we survived our childhood.

This is what's most different. We don't do this anymore. A pile of us don't ride out to Reedy at ten in the morning and fish till sundown. We don't come into the screened-in porch, sunburnt and stinking like cricket guts and fish slime, hauling in a catch that could feed a hundred men. The women don't come out with knives. You don't hear the faucet squeak on. We don't gut and clean the fish, dust them in flour and cornmeal. You don't smell warming grease. There won't be a pile of us huddling, bowing our heads in prayer. You won't see them there. You won't hear them telling stories until midnight. This is what I can never give to you. No matter how good I am, this I can never recreate. And it makes me sad. Because this, little men, is what it meant to me to fish. Gone, in an instant.

For a large part of your life, I've tried to make my childhood yours. My biggest fear was that these things would disappear with me. But they won't. You'll hear me tell their stories, and you'll hear me tell mine, and one day you'll tell your own.

Today when we ride down that dirt road, it's the four of us. We let you drive. We let the dogs chase. I hold your Daddy's hand, and we smile at what we have, at what we've made. The truth is, I'm still growing up here.

"Whose land is this?" I ask.

"Our land!" You say.

"Whose land is this?"

"Our land!"

You'll remember that chant. You'll remember skinny-dipping and cannonballing in rainbows. You'll remember your first ant bed, getting lost in the woods and finding your way back home. You'll remember Gaga and Granddaddy, Wanda and Pam, Bond, and your crazy Uncle Mike. You'll remember him half naked, wearing J.T.'s safari hat with an AK-47 strapped across his back talking about the end times while drinking Kool-Aid and Vodka because he's dieting. You'll remember your Daddy snorkeling the entire pond, scouting for bream beds and bass hidcouts. You'll remember how he always stood in the boat and how he always threw back every fish he ever caught. You'll remember him teaching you to cast. You'll remember catching your first fish, both of you.

Some mornings when you are still asleep in your bunk, I sit on the porch and watch your Daddy fish. I don't know which sight is more reverent, watching you fishing with him or watching him on the water alone. He stands in the boat, casts his line in the mist. Your father walks on water.

I sit and I listen. I hear birdsong and butterfly wings, the slither of a snake. The wind picks up, and I hear them in the pines, the ones who came and left before my birth, the ones I've eulogized and buried. I hear them telling stories.

One day you'll wake up, and I'll be gone. Promise me, little men, you'll keep us alive.

Fishing Lessons
RON RASH

I f you drive on the Blue Ridge Parkway from Blowing Rock to Boone, North Carolina, you will come across a brown sign that reads, "Aho Gap Elevation 3,722 feet." A road comes in from the left side. If you look down that road, you will see a small white farmhouse on the right. My aunt lives there now, but once my grandmother did, and for much of the summer from when I was age eight to seventeen, I lived there as well.

It was a childhood and early adolescence unimaginable today—part Huck Finn and part Fern Hill. My grandmother lived alone, my grandfather dead, her eight children now living elsewhere. There was no vehicle on the farm, and her black-and-white television picked up one channel, on a good day. The closest store was a gas station four miles away. On those summer mornings my grandmother fixed a breakfast of eggs, cathead biscuits with gravy, jam, or butter she churned herself, and milk that came from the Guernsey in the barn. I'd usually wrap up a couple of biscuits in a backpack, fill a canteen my uncle had brought back from the army, and go get my rod and reel. Until I was twelve, when I received a fly rod and reel for Christmas, I'd dig a few worms near the barn. After that it was trout flies or, if I used my spinning rod, Mepps spinners.

I fished several streams, but often I'd walk up the dirt road to the Parkway and go left. Soon I'd come to the headwaters of Goshen Creek. My mother's family has lived in the area since the early 1800s. Important moments in their lives, including one death, have occurred on this stream. When I stepped into Goshen Creek, I entered a current that also ran through time.

But I didn't enter the stream at its headwaters. I walked two miles down the Blue Ridge Parkway to Goshen Creek Bridge. Though I didn't know it at the time, I was preparing myself to become a writer. As I walked, I thought about events in my life and I daydreamed—often inspired by the Parkway's exotic traffic. Over those years I saw license plates from every state in the Union, including Alaska and Hawaii. I learned to recognize tags without glimpsing the state name—Florida with its dark green and Kentucky with its blue. Because I was eighteen before I ever went beyond the boundaries of North and South Carolina, those tags bespoke places I knew only from words and images, lessons from school. As the vehicles passed, I'd remember something I'd learned about that state—Kansas had wheat fields that made waves like oceans; Washington had redwoods and rain; New York had crowds and skyscrapers. I'd think about those things, and place the states on a map I unscrolled in my mind. But mainly I'd imagine what it would be like to visit these places.

When I got to Goshen Creek Bridge, I'd make my way down to the creek. My uncle Howard's cabbage patch bordered this stretch of the stream. I rarely fished here, though, because in the bottomland's slow water I caught only knottyheads and suckers.

Once I moved upstream from the bridge, the creek made an abrupt ascent. Here the creek had scenery pretty enough for calendars and magazines. It was not an easy place to fish, however. The rocks were slippery and no trails lined the banks. The only way upstream was hopping rock to rock or wading. Because of these difficulties and my tending to fish during weekday mornings, I can't remember ever encountering another fisherman once I was above the first big waterfall. I would go hours without seeing another living soul, yet this never bothered me. Even as a small child I'd been comfortable in solitude. Those hours alone on Goshen Creek were yet more preparation for the life of a writer.

For almost a mile, the stream was primarily waterfalls and deep, clear pools. The only fish I ever caught here were rainbows that leaped so high sometimes they would land themselves on rocks or sand. They were sleek and pink-striped, usually eight to twelve inches, the perfect size for eating. I'd put them on my stringer, and my grandmother and I would have them for supper. In the late 1800s, my ancestors built a mill-race in this section of the stream. My great-great-grandfather operated it for several years, but one evening he did not come home. His son found him. He had somehow been caught and then crushed by the great wheel.

Farther upstream the land leveled and the waterfalls were fewer, but there was a trough-shaped pool that, while not large, was particularly deep. I never pulled a lunker trout out of Goshen Creek, but when I was fourteen, it was here that I had my one chance. I was fishing with a

Mepps spinner and cast into the foam at the pool's head. I let the lure sink and then started my retrieve. A trout followed my spinner into the pool's tailwaters. A big trout. A trout bigger than any trout I'd ever seen outside of fishing magazines, too big for such a small stream, but here it was. As big as a salmon, thirty inches at least, or so it seemed. In retrospect, the rainbow would have gone eighteen to twenty inches, not a trophy trout in many places, but it was on a western North Carolina creek. The trout followed until its fin broke the water. Then, just as it looked as if it would inhale the spinner, the fish turned and disappeared back in the pool's depths, where it has stayed for forty-five years.

There are several steps when a fourteen-year-old boy almost snags the biggest fish of his life: (1) Denial. That didn't just happen. That fish was a trick of the light, a hallucination. (2) Yes, it was real, and if you cast again it will strike this time (it didn't). (3) You'll come back tomorrow or next week or next summer and you'll catch it (nope). (4) Given time, years, even decades, you will accept that not catching that fish was part of the cosmic plan (nope).

There were more pools, a good half mile's worth. Then the creek split. One branch veered left and the other continued close to the Parkway. It was at this fork, during the Civil War, where another ancestor, a young mountain woman, encountered a wounded Union soldier while washing clothes. The soldier begged for her help and she gave it, providing food and protection until, with the help of her uncle, a Union sympathizer, she was able to lead him back safely into Tennessee and behind Union lines.

I followed Goshen Creek's smaller fork to the left. There were no more rainbows. Instead, there were only brook trout, although everyone I knew called them speckled trout or specks. These were the only trout (technically a char) native to southern Appalachia. They lived in only the purest water and did not compete well with browns and rainbows.

These were small fish but the most beautiful, their flanks dotted with olive, gold, and red—dorsal fins as orange as fireweed. As I got older, I felt guilty about taking them from the creek to eat. By my mid-teens I no longer did.

After a few hundred more yards, the creek came out of the gorge and ran alongside the Parkway. The waterfalls and pools disappeared, replaced by slower water often cloaked in mountain laurel. When the stream became too small to hold anything more than fingerlings, I stepped out of the water and walked along the grass beside the Parkway, soaked feet to knees. Fishing the gorge usually took the whole morning, so there were times I would sit on the bank and eat the ham or jelly biscuits I'd brought with me. I'd watch the cars go by, and think of the magical places they came from and would return to.

I turn sixty years old this year. If I could go back in time, and talk to that solitary boy sitting on the Parkway grass, I would tell him this— though you can't imagine it now, there will come a time when you will travel to these places you dream of, and not just other states but other continents as well, and you will look back on your life and know the happiest, most amazing place that you have ever found was here.

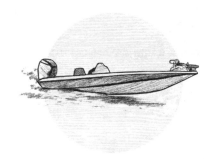

In Lightning Past
M.O. WALSH

The fish that saw us were not impressed. Who could blame them?

We thought we were smart, my buddy Brock and me; a couple of writers in grad school skipping class to fish a place called Spring Lake. It sat along Hwy 7, off a pale stretch of road between Oxford and Holly Springs, and it seemed nobody fished it but us. This was north Mississippi, circa 2004. I was near thirty, still rocking a full head of hair and just married. My buddy Brock was younger, maybe twenty five, but had already been married for a fifth of his life and therefore looked as old as me in his way. We had our tackle and poles and our beer and my boat and had each hauled in enough fish in our day to have stories, to have techniques. But we had never seen this.

"Look at them," Brock said, and thumped a can of Skoal with his finger. "They're just staring at us."

Two big largemouth bass, hog legs, we liked to call them, sat floating beside our boat in plain sight. They were maybe a foot deep in the water and hovered next to a tangle of roots, both facing the same way, as if expecting a bus. They looked close enough to shake hands with and their exhibitionism unnerved us. Based on our previous experience at Spring Lake, which we'd fished nearly twice a week that past year, this felt like spotting a couple of Yetis.

I cast out a jig to see what would happen. It sank as quiet and quick as a dream, but the problem was that we could see it, just as clearly as we could see the fish we were trying to catch. Nothing had ever looked as artificial to me as my bait in that moment; the black metal head, grey wire skirt, green rubber tail, the red hook. It resembled neither the living nor the dead. I might as well have dropped in a radio. My cast missed the larger one by less than an inch but neither fish bothered to move. No strike of hunger, no strike in self-defense, no flash of color as they high tailed for cover. They instead seemed preoccupied, almost philosophical, as if above the entire charade.

"Well," I said. "This is atypical."

On the map of our lives, we'd met in the middle, me and Brock. I'm from South Louisiana and he's from East Tennessee, so we were somewhat equidistant from home there in North Mississippi. Since our schoolmates were from places like Philly and NYC, Brock and I bonded over our collective Southernness, if that is a word. Yet we still had our differences. I was raised Catholic and he was raised Baptist. I was more Swamp Pop and he was more Country. What this meant is that I would say, "Come on, man, let's have another drink. Let's get tooted," and he would check his phone to see if his wife had texted him to go home and let out the dog or mow the lawn and then say, "Nah, I probably shouldn't," but then have six more. All to say that we took different routes to the same destination and understood each other well. We were friends.

I reeled in my line as Brock changed his lure.

"I don't know, buddy," he said. "It might be a long day."

I cast again.

"Maybe if I can hit one on the mouth," I said. "He'll just kind of breathe it in."

To understand my frustration with this water, you should know that where I grew up you don't see what you've caught until it's landed. If you're in the salt or the marsh or the Gulf, the water is so often dark and choppy and large that you could pull up any number of surprises: a speck or a red or a flounder, maybe even a turtle. You could pull up something ancient with teeth that you'd still gut and fry if the size was right. Even in our rivers and lakes, the water is silted to the color of chocolate milk and you can't see what goes on down there. You likely don't want to know. Brock was used to clearer waters in Tennessee, sure, water you might even be tempted to drink, but rushing by him so fast in the creeks and streams that he'd waded, casting flies to land fish so handsome and sleek he couldn't help but release them, that this still-water clarity was new to him, too. His were the kind of fish you pull from swirls and take pictures of, not for their weight or ferocity, but for the way sunlight glints off their skin like a prism, for the way they already look like a picture.

We'd fished the bass of Spring Lake plenty that year, putting around every inch of it in my john boat, trolling across the big blank slate of its middle, pushing ourselves through the clusters of cypress and mangroves that edged its banks. We'd run buzzbaits and flukes and poppers.

We'd dropped worms and jigs and more jigs. We'd rigged Texas and Carolina and had, what felt to us like, plans for every occasion. But the lake appeared transformed since we last came across it, it had been purified in some way, and so we poked around our brains for the reasons. Had there been rain lately? There had, we remembered. Pouring rain. Maybe that was it. Enough rain to turn the lake to a bath.

Brock stood up and took in the scene. "Look over there," he said, and nodded toward a circle of trees ahead. "Three more," he told me. "Hog legs, too."

I clicked on the small motor as Brock cast about and I looked down into the lake as we trolled. I could see the bottom as clear as I saw my own hands. Every once in a while, though, I noticed a strange thing; a sliver of gold, it looked like, a toothpick set atop the grey dirt of the lake floor. I saw one and then another. I checked the other side of the boat and saw the same thing. Five or six of them, easy, some as long as a pencil, all of them sharpened to points and facing the same direction.

"Are you seeing this?" Brock asked me.

I clicked off the motor and stood, figuring maybe his line had gotten snagged in a tree, but he had stopped casting altogether. In front of us now, a field of golden slivers. They were uniform in their arrangement, as if the outward rays of a sunken sun we could not see, and the closer we got to the stand of cypress ahead of us the denser they became. We passed fish standing so still below us that I could see the easy work of their gills.

"What the hell are they?" Brock said, and I knew what it was that he wanted. We were no longer looking for fish. I sat back at the motor and made it hum slow. We coasted like hunters over the new landscape beneath us, the brightening bottom of the lake bed, and found a path into the cluster of trees.

"God, man," Brock said, and we saw it.

In the middle of the circle of trees, a cypress so gold as to dull all the colors around it. The top had been shorn off completely, relieved of its limbs and bark, and the remaining trunk stood as proud as a sword. At its base, the water as clear as new glass.

"Lightning," Brock said, and the probable past unfolded.

In the night, perhaps, sometime that we were not looking, that we were not there, an explosion so powerful as to have killed anything that was. All of those golden slivers, we now knew, were not slivers but splinters, arrows, darts that would have shot into our bodies like needles. The power of it, the awful beauty. We did not speak for a time, and we did not fish.

Instead we looked up at the neighboring trees, where huge golden limbs sat snagged in their branches. Wood as large as human legs hung tangled above us, all glowing and undeniably new. We became amateur sleuths in our heads, wondering how long ago it could have happened, what it would have felt like to be there the moment it did, and how widespread the damage could be. We took the boat out of the trees and trolled circles around the point of impact.

"Another one over here," I said, "and here," and the last one we saw, finally, more than a hundred yards away from the strike. We traded scientific theories, me and Brock, our poles planked between the seats of the boat. What sort of velocity were we dealing with? What frightening speed? And then a strange notion we had both heard in school, long ago, about how lightning actually starts on the ground. It is some sort of disagreement between positive and negative energy, we remembered, recognized by a passing storm, and then corrected without discussion. What we had seen, we both knew, was a place where lightning began.

When I think back about this now, and the way we acted for the rest of that day, I wonder if the ghosts of those needles got in us. We left the lake and loaded the boat and took off down the road as if high. We guzzled beers and called up friends and retold the story to ourselves again and again. We went to the store and bought more beer, a bottle of bourbon, and thick-as-your-fist steaks. We were going back to Brock's to eat well, by God, to drink heartily, to let out the dog, and to pet him like we hadn't seen him in months. We were never going to sleep. And then the years went by and Brock would find out about another man in his wife's life and he would go on to find another love and then another after that and our professors would die or become famous and our friends would write books and enter rehab and either birth or miscarry children. For my part, I would go on to stay married and raise children of my own and after a year of noticing strange symptoms find myself in a hospital room with my wife as a doctor asks if she can feel what he is doing on her left side as strongly as what he is doing on her right and the answer she gives me with only a look, the sudden way our steady lives would be rendered fragile and new, will blow me to bits, and I will be reminded of those golden splinters.

The power. The awful beauty. The phrase itself. *The place where lightning began* became and remains a refrain for me and Brock even now as we try to puzzle out the current state of our lives, how we got here, if we are happy, and what we can do to control that which is so obviously bigger than us. We still speak of it often, on the phone, late at night; the pattern of gold on the lake bottom, the clarity of the water, the stunned fish floating reverent below.

Yet what I remember most is this: We were young. We were friends. We were fishing. We had unknowable futures before us and had seen something, that day, that no one else had seen. We were naïve. We were unprepared. And though we had little money we felt so tremendously grand, so thankful for what we had witnessed, for what it felt like we had somehow survived and could speak about, could even live on for a while if we had to, that, when it came time to eat, we threw an extra steak on the grill for the dog.

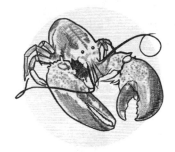

Lobstering With Griff
INGRID THOFT

L obsters don't come out of the sea with bright red shells and claws bound by thick rubber bands. It was only as a tween, when I went lobstering with my friend, Griff, on a humid summer day, that the truth about lobsters was revealed.

Griff kept his boat tied up to the dock next to his house, and we'd set out to pull his pots that hugged the coast of Marblehead, Massachusetts. Idling next to a buoy, the boat rocked gently as he showed me how to hoist the Styrofoam marker and the rope into the boat, the large unwieldy pot not far behind. If luck was on our side, we'd find a few dark greenish specimens in the structure's netting. One of us would hold the

lobsters—with their claws waving in the air they looked like small mae-
stros searching for a tempo—and the other would put the bands in place.

My friendship with Griff was forged in afternoons on the water, but
it all started with a paper route that took me around the neighborhood
every afternoon. A talkative kid who liked to meet the neighbors, I would
dawdle along the route. It would often take more than an hour to finish,
given that I had to check in with my customers and collect the occasional treat.

Griff and Mrs. Griff—a well-known couple in the neighborhood in
their sixties—were just beyond the halfway point on my travels and my
favorite stop on my route. Their house was down a steep flight of stairs,
perched on the water, and I'd always find Mrs. Griff in the kitchen, and
Griff in his recliner next to the window that overlooked the harbor. He
had binoculars and a police scanner; nothing would happen on his
watch without his knowledge. We'd catch up on the day's news, and
then I'd finally climb the stairs to the street and finish unloading my
canvas bag of papers.

Griff and I began to take on projects, and I found that my neighborhood lobsterman was mischievous and delighted in surprising me. In
addition to lobstering, he had a large vegetable garden, which seemed to
claim ever more square footage in the yard every season. He grew pump-
kins, and one October, I was thrilled to find a large pumpkin on our
doorstep, my nickname, Iggy, writ large on the orange surface. Griff had
used a knife and written my name on a baby pumpkin, only to have it
grow, the letters stretching across the surface. I posed proudly for a picture with the gift. I had spent my childhood searching through "Irenes"
and "Isaacs" in the displays of tiny license plates and souvenir bracelets,
never finding an "Ingrid." It was magical to receive such a unique, per-
sonalized item, and it was a squash! Who got their own squash?

At one point, I expressed an interest in having my own garden, and

Griff and I hatched a plan to cultivate a small square of soil between the street and my front yard. We planted tomatoes and peppers, and I tended them faithfully, watering when required, and weeding as needed. But patience has never been my strong suit, and every day I would check the plants, eager to see some progress. I was always disappointed; where were the large, red tomatoes and the glossy peppers that had been promised on the seed packets? What more was I supposed to do other than wait, for which I had no capacity?

One morning, I came outside and did my cursory review of the small garden only to be stunned by what I found. The vines bowed under the weight of ripe tomatoes and peppers: I'd finally reaped a bounty! I took a step into the plot, pushing aside green tendrils, and was puzzled by what I found. Near the ready-to-eat veggies were baby versions, green and not quite fully formed. Upon closer inspection, I found that the ripe vegetables were tied on to the vine with green twist ties, the product of more mature vines in some other garden. I informed my parents of the development. They claimed innocence. That left only one possible suspect. I called Griff and thanked him for bolstering my belief in my farming skills, if only temporarily.

A peculiarity of my childhood neighborhood was that a small AM radio station broadcast out of a former house across the street. There was a field surrounding the radio tower, which by the way, Griff had climbed clandestinely as a young man. Griff knew the staff well and wondered if I might like a job there. Apparently, he felt my chatty disposition was well suited to radio work, and on his recommendation, I was offered a job working the 5-8 a.m. shift. The early hour felt brutal to my fifteen-year-old self, and I would leave the radio station each morning and head straight to a YMCA camp counselor job with four-to-six-year-olds. It was an exhausting schedule, but I loved working at the radio station.

A shoestring operation, the radio station was run by a small, but loyal staff, and I was shown the ropes and allowed to do just about everything. I found stories on the AP wire, called local police departments to check if there'd been any news overnight—there never was—and did segments on-air. I still cringe when I remember mangling the baseball highlights, but I realized by the end of the summer that every sports quote was the same: "I just put the bat on the ball/stick on the puck/ball in the hoop and get the job done."

I got some fan mail and calls from the largely elderly audience, and one day, I started getting mail from other parts of the United States. The writer would recall being in the area and hearing my outstanding broadcasting. He or she just had to let me know how wonderful I was. Years of Griff's hijinks had honed my BS detector and after I'd received a handful of letters, he admitted that he was the writer. A commercial pilot in the neighborhood had been kind enough to mail the notes and cards from his stops across the country. Griff had even gone so far as to try and disguise his handwriting; if I didn't look too closely, I could almost believe I had a transcontinental following.

I saw less of Griff as I got older, but he always seemed to know what was going on and had an opinion on it. Sophomore year of college I was dating my now-husband, and we'd often spend the weekends at my childhood home, where my parents no longer lived full-time. My husband drove a bright yellow Jeep, and it occupied a prime spot in the driveway when we were there. One afternoon, Griff called and said he was so sorry that my boyfriend was having car trouble and needed to spend the night so often. Griff would be happy to come over and troubleshoot, say, take a look at the engine, so as to get my boyfriend safely back on the road. I thanked him for his concern, but reassured him that the car was in fine working order.

But it was lobstering with Griff—bobbing in the Atlantic, learning to pull pots, no matter that I was a girl and this wasn't usually a job for girls—that comes to mind when I think of my neighborhood buddy. When you grow up in New England, you learn that lobster isn't for the fainthearted. They may be relatively easy to lure into the trap on the ocean floor, but they put up a fight when you pull them out and snap the bands on their claws.

After pulling traps with Griff, I would walk home with some of the crustaceans in a bag, wriggling and emitting a sharp salty tang. My sisters and I would each choose a competitor and then let them loose on the kitchen floor to race. The participants were never focused—crawling off in this direction and that—and the event was a meandering affair that lasted until the water was boiling. Helping my mom drop the lobsters into a pot of scalding water and watching their shells change to bright red never fazed me. How would we enjoy their rich flesh if we didn't kill them first?

Eating a lobster is a messy proposition, and to the uninitiated, freeing the succulent meat is a puzzle. Lobsters make you work for their bounty. You have to crack open claws—as soft as paper or as hard as rock depending upon when you catch them in molting season. You can't be put off by the green tomalley between the tail and the upper body, although like me, you may choose to slide the liver substance onto your mother's plate. The coral-colored roe (black before it's cooked) is another substance lurking in the body that some diners find delectable. Again, another donation for my mother.

Although I'm not a fan of those parts of the lobster, they don't put me off my meal, not like dinner guests we once had who looked stricken when crustaceans were put before them. The wife was so distressed by the presentation she needed to lie down. Granted, she was pregnant, however a pregnant New Englander wouldn't think twice when faced with the beady eyed creature. She would pull off the claws, twist the body apart, remove the center fin on the end of the tail and shove her finger up the lobster's tail, thereby releasing the largest—and some say tastiest—hunk of meat.

When I return to Massachusetts every August, an image of Griff always comes to mind. On warm sunny days in my childhood, Griff would peel himself away from the police scanner, and I'd find him working in the garden or maybe sitting by the front door taking a breather. He'd be in a plastic folding chair, the kind made from interwoven strips of nylon and a silver metal frame.

"Iggy!" he'd holler, waving a grubby hand in the air.

We'd visit, and I was often sent home with fresh veggies, a batch of Mrs. Griff's blueberry muffins, a few lobsters.

These days, I tend to get my lobsters pre-cooked. We pick them up at the local fish market—next to the dock where the lobster boats come in each morning—in an insulated bag full of red shells and briny steam, and I'm reminded of the bounty that was my friendship with Griff. When I snap open a lobster claw or pry the meat from the tail, I'm rewarded with sweet flavor and the memories of a man who sat across from me in a rocking dory, giving me a glimpse of what life had to offer.

The Mullet Girls
JILL MCCORKLE

very summer my family spent a week at the beach—for
years going to the same house at Holden Beach, N.C.
This house had (pre-Hurricane Hazel, 1954) been set
back from the ocean a couple of rows but now in the late '60s
and early '70s was oceanfront, high tide reaching and lapping beneath the wooden steps leading up to the screened-in
porch. My dad's best friend, who owned the house, continued
to pay a meager amount of property tax (seventy-odd cents
a year) on the land that was already submerged. In spite of
many efforts, sandbags and sea oats, the ocean has continued

to devour this small part of the world such that what I remember is far removed from what now remains.

I had just turned thirteen and for the first time was dividing my days between my mom and older sister, who liked to swim and sun read, and my dad, who spent the entire day either fishing or getting ready to fish. The house was full of people that summer, various friends and relatives, our teenage boy cousins we didn't see very often. We spent a lot of time playing cards, our cousins' united goal being to get us to say "the ace of spades," which sent them into convulsive laughter about how we sounded just like we had stepped out of *The Andy Griffith Show*. They were, after all, from Maryland, which was the North by our standards.

Out of the blue on one of those afternoons, two women in bikini tops and short shorts appeared at the screen door. They called out my father's name in shrill girlish yoo-hoos. "Johnny! Oh, Johnny!"

We all froze. Even though the whole exchange took only a few minutes, it became the event of the week and one we referred to often for years after. We called them the Bathing Beauties, the Beach Walkers, the Mullet Girls.

Any other year and I would not have been the one to go to the door. I would have been with my dad fishing. I was his fishing buddy (or at least he allowed me to think that); his surrogate son. I prided myself on being the daughter who could touch anything stinky and slimy without flinching. I reached into the rich loamy earth and plucked my own fat squirmy bloodworm from the plastic carton. I speared, twisted, and looped it on my hook, wiped the blood and goo on the butt of my swimsuit. I had spent hours learning how to cast, my thumb poised and ready to slow the momentum smoothly instead of giving it a jerk that would result in my dad having to sit and unwrap and untangle—something he had already done many, many times.

Once we caught a spiney sharp-toothed fish, his struggling mouth like serrated scissors. It looked prehistoric, spiked and dangerous, and

I am still not sure to this day what kind of fish it was. My dad gave up trying to extract the bloody hook where it was firmly wedged and simply cut the line up close and tossed the creature back into the surf. "Poor old fella," he said, "his wife is going to be so disappointed when he gets home." Just the way he said it with such conviction and compassion left me saddened for the rest of the day as I imagined that silver briny body cutting its way against the tide, the hook already rusting. All day I saw him swimming out into the coldest, darkest depths in search of his mate.

The women at the door were as surprised to see all of us as we were to see them. I just stood and stared at them through the dark mesh of the screen. I had seen them earlier as I rocked on the porch and used the binoculars to spot dolphins and the large shrimp boats that were always hovering on the horizon. I had watched them strolling back and forth on the beach, bending to pick up shells in a way that made their shorts ride up even higher. They had stopped several times and peered into the yellow bucket beside my dad's sand chair, which we had just given him for Father's Day, curious about his catch. I knew there was probably nothing in the bucket. I knew that he often stopped baiting his hook so that he had an excuse to sit and stare at the ocean.

What I had seen from a distance as the Mullet Girls strolled back and forth were two bronzed bodies in bikinis. Up close they were not at all what I had expected.

"Is Johnny here?" the one with the bobby pinned rollers hidden up under her scarf asked. I did not like the sound of his name coming out of her mouth. It made me mad. It made me feel just as I had as a six-year-old, when, after seeing, *The Sound of Music*, my dad commented on how pretty he thought Julie Andrews was. I worried for the next few months that my parents would leave each other for Julie Andrews and Christopher Plummer, and there I'd be with eight siblings instead of one. My sister would do okay; she could sing. But where would I ever fit in with that crew?

"Well, is he still fishing somewhere?" This was the short one, her hair bleached to a shade of yellow that would only be considered natural on an egg yolk. She closed one eye against the trail of smoke from the cigarette she held in the corner of her mouth. Her hands, I noticed, were clutching a big canvas bag.

"He's not here," I said, hoping that my cousins were hearing their accents, slow and flat even to my ear. The folks from Mayberry sounded like British royalty by comparison. "And I'm not sure where he is."

"Well, you tell him we were by," the short one said. "He'll know who you mean. We promised him some mullet if we had some luck, and, boy, did we have some luck."

"We'll stop by after dark," the other one said, and I stood and watched as they walked down the road to an old blue Chevrolet.

I knew exactly where my dad was. Every day, later afternoon, low, tide, he walked way down the beach to what connected the ocean to the inland waterway. At low tide we could walk across the channel and find live starfish and sand dollars and conchs along the way. He could sit there for hours, just watching the water, tending his fishing pole, puffing on his pipe, sipping a beer. He liked to think about all that he would do when his ship came in—a long, long list—only to make his way back around to say that things were pretty good the way that they were, he really wouldn't want to change a whole lot. Maybe he'd ask for two weeks' vacation from his job at the post office instead of one.

He talked about depression long before it was an acceptable thing to talk about, taking great solace in the knowledge that both Lincoln and Churchill had been fellow sufferers. He also found a way to put a positive spin on that condition, saying about at least one acquaintance, "I don't know that I think this fella is smart enough to be depressed." He told me how some of the greatest moments of his life were when he fished with my mother's father long before he had married into the family. How my grandfather had tied a rope to his belt, the other end to a sack of beers which he allowed to roll and wash under the waves where it was cool.

For years my dad had entrusted me with a special assignment. When he left for the point, he handed me an alarm clock with strict instructions that when the alarm sounded I should run to the refrigerator and grab the brown paper bag and run as fast as I could down to his special fishing spot. For a long time I thought I was carrying bait, the bait that would land the huge fish that had just gotten away. What I ultimately discovered was that in those pre-Playmate cooler days, I was making a beer run—two iced Falstaffs wrapped in aluminum foil and swaddled in paper towels in the paper sack. I was a two-legged Saint Bernard. I was part of a legacy my maternal grandfather had started. My dad fancied the idea of Smoky, our black shepherd mix who hated anyone who was not in our immediate family, with a keg on his neck, but by then he had his cooler. And he still had me.

"Who were they?" my mother asked. "Have you ever seen such skimpy outfits?" If there was a flush to her cheeks, it was well concealed by her annual sunburn. Fair and freckled, she was trying to get a tan even if it meant the occasional burn and a dowsing of QT lotion. "And what did they want with Johnny?"

I told her how up close they looked nothing like they did from a distance. They were odd looking. Coarse. Rough and worn out. They were wrinkled like old prunes and they smelled fishy.

"Something's fishy," she said, and though I knew it was a joke, I found it hard to laugh. I kept thinking how she had said, "What did they want with Johnny?" Not your daddy, but Johnny, leaving me to feel left out the same way I did when I looked at photographs before I was born: a young family of three, or before my sister; a couple of newlyweds. They had known each other their whole lives; they had dated since they were sixteen. They had been married for twenty years and were in their early forties, and it was the first time since "The Sound of Music" that I had ever really thought of them as people who might attract others, or worse, be attracted to another, especially another who did not resemble Julie Andrews in the slightest.

"One of them had her hair rolled up," I said. "Where's she going, Surfside or Van Werry's?"—the one and only grocery store down near the drawbridge. Everybody else just laughed and went back to playing spades. There was nowhere to go in that neck of the woods other than Surfside Pavilion, a squat, pink cinderblock building with two pool tables and a few pinball machines and a miniature golf course that was always soggy and warped from years of damp salt air and rain.

I had seen girls hanging out of car windows hooting and hollering at boys who stood around outside the pavilion smoking cigarettes and waxing their surfboards. My mother liked to use loud girls who hung out of car windows with cigarettes in their mouths and breasts spilling from tight bathing suits as examples of what not to grow up and be.

"Don't you ever let me catch you looking like that," my mother said.

"So should we hide?" my sister asked without cracking a smile. She was sixteen and had far more clout than I did.

We had heard all the stories about what girls NOT to be like. It was for this very reason that we had stopped going to Ocean Drive and Myrtle Beach, which had become a haven for teenagers and college kids who wanted to party, have sex, fall into violent and drunken sidewalk brawls, and enter the shag contests at places like The Pad and the Spanish Galleon, where the music of the Tams and the Drifters and Maurice Williams and the Zodiacs blasted all through the night. People said that you could go to South Carolina and get married, get a drink or two, buy some fireworks, get a divorce and still be home in time for the eleven o'clock news.

Surfside Pavilion paled by comparison, but we had gotten used to it. The quiet; the women like my mother who, if they wore a swimsuit at all, wore a one-piece with boy legs or little skirts. Suits that hid all evidence that children had ever sprung from their bodies.

That summer I wore bikinis and I was working on my tan and spraying lemon juice into my hair as "Glamour" magazine suggested, more than I was fishing. I braided my long hair into pigtails and wore a beaded headband. I wore a large silver peace sign strung on a piece of rawhide (both items I had purchased at the pier after reading all the dirty postcards that were prominently displayed on a revolving rack). My sister spent most of the late afternoons strumming her guitar and singing Joan Baez and Bob Dylan songs. She wrapped her guitar in a blanket and placed it on the empty bottom bunk below me so that the salt air wouldn't damage it. Her boyfriend had driven down to see her a couple of days earlier, then a couple of friends came by with some friends who brought some friends and so on. My mom said that she didn't like how one of those boys looked at me, with me barely thirteen years old, and that even if I had wanted to tag along and walk down the beach with them when asked she would not let me.

"Somebody was looking at me that way?" I asked again. After all, I would never wear that beaded headband once I got home and the fire engine nail polish would come off, too. I didn't mind hearing that I had been looked at; I just didn't want to hear it from my mom. And I did want to know just what had led him to look at me. What had I said that might have lured his attention? That I really like Cat Stevens's song "Wild World," that I had been to a Steppenwolf concert? Or was it that I was still on those hot late afternoons willing to go down to the point to crab, dragging a stinking, half-rotten fish head behind me.

And now here were the Mullet Girls—live and in Technicolor. This wasn't a picture of a couple of young wild beach babes. This was the after picture: the wild young girls who got old quick after a lot of fast and rough living. Bad men and bad marriages. The flat, tired eyes, the smear of cheap lipstick, the way that they seemed to crane their necks to look longingly into the cottage where my mother sat in her long shorts, hair blown back from her smooth, clean face. The Mullet Girls made me stop and look at my mother in a whole new way.

They did return later that night, long after my dad had come home with an empty bucket, long after the last boiled shrimp was eaten and we were all out on the porch—no lights so we could see the stars and the flash of the beacon from the Fort Caswell lighthouse. At high tide the waves lapped up under the house, the beginning of a cycle that would—over the next twenty years—claim all of the shore where all of this took place. My own adolescent Atlantis.

The Mullet Girls arrived in fancy white slacks rolled up so that they didn't get wet, spiny spiked-heel sandals swinging from their fingers. The blonde carried the sack, this time held away from her low-cut silky blouse. They were definitely dressed for an evening out. They came with a gift of mullets and who knows what else had they not found an entire family perched in the dark.

My dad politely opened the door and invited them in while I held tight to Smoky's collar. The blond put one bare foot forward and then stopped short when she saw us there.

"Oh my," she laughed nervously and looked over to get her friend's reaction. "You all look like a bunch of owls up here." They both watched my dad, who flipped the switch of the yellow bulb beside the door. She handed him the bag of mullets, which he graciously accepted even though I knew that he would toss them in the freezer below for the next visitor. He wasn't going to clean them and I knew my mother wasn't. He turned and introduced us all—his wife, his kids, his dog. By then their speech was animated, their polite nods to us stiff and hurried. And then they were going—over to the Blockade Runner at Wrightsville Beach, where there was a comedy show—cover charge covered two of your drinks, they said. They wiggled off in a cloud of cologne and whiskey-voiced giggles and we never saw them again.

The Mullet Girls. Temptation had come knocking on our door and my dad, with gentle Southern kindness, had more or less said, *thank you very much but no thanks*. I know they had been hoping for a different scenario, and I often pictured them returning home from vacation to dark and cold places, imagining how different their lives might be if they had ever landed someone like my dad. How different it might be if that stretch of the coast had not been gradually washed over by the ocean, and if parents never got older, never got sick, never died. There are times when I hear an alarm clock, and before I can pull myself up and through the years I am thinking "grab the bag, grab the bag," and then I am off and running down to the point, fine white sand sifting under my feet. I am only thirteen; my dad is forty-two.

The Simple Angle(r)
ERIK STOREY

When you grow up in landlocked areas, especially those in the arid high deserts of the West, you tend to develop a kinship with any water you happen to find. If you spend enough time on the shores, then that kinship will eventually evolve into an all-out love affair. It happened to me at a young age. I fell in love with the White River as soon as my family moved to its shore when I was four. I learned to swim in the eddies of the White's mostly brown water. Later, when rafting two hundred miles of the Green River, I fell head over heels for the wide, dark waters. And now, living in Grand Junction, Colorado, next to the mighty river our state is named after, I designate whole days to walk along and stare at its waters with the same warm longing of a lover.

What's any of this have to do with fishing, you may ask? Simple. For all the thousands of hours that I've spent on, in, or near water, I can count on two hands and ten toes the times I've cast a lure or fly or bait into those waters as an adult. The reason? Not because I dislike fishing; not at all. Tossing a line is perhaps the most relaxing and Zen-like experience I've had. But the reason I don't do it much is because I'm an awful fisherman. Horrendous. I've never had the patience to stand and cast. If I'm by the water I love, it doesn't take long before I'm either swimming or I'm hiking along the shore, looking for birds and the strange insects that reside there.

This lack of patience is also the reason I'm so bad at the actual baiting, casting, reeling, and catching of fish. Because I never took the time to learn properly, and it was completely my own fault. My dad took me fishing many, many times, and almost every time I'd get frustrated and throw my rod down in disgust and go tramping somewhere out in the woods behind the water in search of something more adventurous.

I'm still that way. Modern fishing is one of the most complex and confusing outdoor sports on Earth. Millions of lures and flies and baits for a few hundred species of fish. Even more rod and reel options. Then there are the tactics, which would make even an every-day-for-forty-years fisherman feel like an educated apprentice, waiting to break out to journeyman status. What seems so simple from the outside is too complicated for someone like me.

But, there's a reason for this, too. There was a fishing trip, an epic one I took as a youth that showed me both how humans devolve and how fishing doesn't need to be like this. How it can be a simple connection between the water and the fish and yourself. It turned out to be the greatest fishing experience I've ever had.

I was maybe ten years old, and was given the honor of being invited to go with my father and his friends on an early summer fishing and camping trip in the Flattops Wilderness. I saw it as a chance to learn and earn respect from the men, and was so excited the week before the trip I barely slept. I barely ate. I bounced with happiness and excitement in the passenger seat as we drove two hours, twisting and slipping our way up to the trailhead.

Upon arrival, I still couldn't contain my excitement and got reprimanded by the elders when my jubilation spooked the packhorses, one of which, I later found out, was there solely to pack the booze and mixers into the middle of nowhere. Or, more accurately, into Marvine Lakes, two of the biggest natural lakes deep inside the designated wilderness.

This was nearly thirty years ago, but I can still remember the blur of greenery, the smell of sweaty horses and blooming lupine, the sounds of the rushing spring waters of the creek, the clicking of horseshoes on granite, and the as-yet-unheard profanities from the men. Unfortunately we never made it to our original destination. Though it was summer in the town we'd left, it was barely spring that high up in the mountains. So we turned the horses around when the snow became too deep and headed back down the trail to set up camp beside a group of small crystal-clear natural lakes.

The next morning our fishing began in earnest. As the sun crept over the cliffs that rimmed the flat-topped mesas to the east, the men headed to the largest of the lakes to cast flies and try their luck. I had other plans. Though only ten, I was completely comfortable wandering the woods alone, and my dad encouraged it, so I grabbed my small Boy Scout daypack and headed to another lake far from the others.

It wasn't until I hit the edge of the clear water that I remembered I didn't bring a fishing pole. Or bait. Or any tackle. *Good thing I'm in the Boy Scouts*, I thought, remembering the small survival kit in the bottom of my pack. Taking it to the water's edge, I carefully untangled the fishing line and attached the single small hook to one end. The other I tied around the longest, straightest pine branch I could find. Stuck the single sinker six inches above it and thought about the bait I didn't have.

I didn't have a shovel either and after a few minutes of digging in the soft black soil with a smaller stick, I gave up looking for worms. Almost gave up on my attempt to salvage the fishing day but remembered something I'd read in one of the survival books I'd perused over the last couple years.

I searched at least five rotting logs until I found what I was looking for—a fat, wriggling, little grub—then spent another half-hour trying to stab the little bugger onto the hook. When I'd baited the hook, I walked over to the edge of the water, noticing the trout darting in the glassy cold water, and tried to cast the improvised line.

The results were disastrous. The limp line lackadaisically fluttered up, and wrapped itself around a low-hanging branch that I hadn't noticed before the cast. I could have given up then and walked back to camp, but it would have been too big of a ding to my boyish pride to return to a fishing camp without a fish. So I spent the next hour or so untangling my "survival" line. This involved me climbing the tree, ripping my hands, and getting a goodly amount of needles down the back of my collar.

But I did somehow manage to get the thing untangled and ready for a second cast. This time, I thought, would be better. I surveyed the trees and brush, making sure nothing would stand in the way of my second try. Checked the hook, and realized the grub had fallen off during the tree incident. That set me back another thirty minutes while I searched and searched and couldn't find any more. Went back to digging and twenty more minutes later finally found a small worm.

Now I was completely ready for the perfect attempt. I was feeling pretty cocky then, already thinking of the brookie or cutthroat this try would catch and how happy my dad and his friends would be when I brought it back to camp. I could see the big spotted fish swimming around the sunken fallen trees in the perfectly clear water, and thought how easy it would be. I'd mostly fished in brown water, waiting for a bobber to move and realized how much simpler it would be now that I could see them hit the bait.

I wouldn't get a chance to find out, however. During my perfect, father-pleasing cast, the stick flew out of my hands and my whole rig soared, then fell, into the lake. The fish I'd been salivating over fled to their respective hidey-holes. I stared at the water for a minute or two, watching a muskrat weave its way around my floating pole and past it to the other side of the pond, where it dragged its soggy body onto solid ground and disappeared. Then I sat down and may or may not have shed a tear or two over my absolute failure. This is where I should have finally given up and gone on to explore the trails in the woods.

But I couldn't bring myself to do it. Couldn't imagine coming back to camp empty handed, when all of the other men would come tromping back with stringers of tasty trout. They would see me as just a little boy, and that would be unacceptable. Only one option left. I pulled out my trusty little Buck knife and found the longest stick laying on the duff. Whittled the tip to a sharp point as I watched chipmunks chase each other in the high trees. Sat and marveled at the dragon and damselflies skimming the translucent water. Finished my makeshift spear while I stared at an abandoned beaver lodge on the far end of the lake, wondering what it looked like on the inside.

Hunger got the best of me before I could try my hand at spear fishing. I dug a couple of granola bars out of my pack and ate them while I waited for the trout to come out and start feeding again. When they did I sat for God-knows how long watching them with the same rapt attention now only afforded to kids when deep in the middle of a Call of Duty game. I studied their patterns, and what they were feeding on. The ripples from their breaching spread across the smooth surface of the pond. My ten-year-old brain overloaded when I tried to figure out why some of the little waves disappeared when they interacted and others changed course or grew in size.

Shaking my hurting head, I stood and readied myself to stab a ticket to acceptance in camp. Wandered over to a deep hole where I'd seen the biggest fish lounging and stood still, noticing the water striders streak away when they saw me. Raised the long spear and shoved it down at the biggest brookie.

I missed, of course. Despite the Scouts, and the books, and my schooling, I had yet to learn how refraction works. The fish scattered and I wandered around the banks of the lake waiting for another opportunity to stick a trout. As I waited, I shivered in the shade and shadows that I hadn't noticed were growing. I watched the clear water turn blue and then a darker emerald, and knew I'd go home empty handed. The fish might have still been there, but with the changing light I couldn't see them and my heart sank as low as the disappearing sun.

I threw the spear away to float in the same lake that had taken my pole, and realized the water had taken more from me than I'd pulled from it. I felt like a failure. Walked away back to camp wiping young tears from my cheeks, anticipating the jokes and derision of older men, but they never came. The men were busy with their own recollections of the day and were already telling stories about what they'd done. It was then, as we sat around a fire to eat good vittles and laugh, I realized none of the campfire conversations centered on fish. The men told war stories, talked about past adventures, and that's when I knew it didn't matter if we had physical trophies—such as fish—to take home. What truly mattered were the memories of the day.

Now, when I get the rare opportunity to go cast a line, and someone sneers at my spincast reel and sewing-kit sized tackle box, I can smile and laugh. Because I learned early what every good angler knows deep down, that it's not the fish, or the gear that makes fishing so addicting, it's the immersive experience in a serene and wonderful environment. And it's those experiences that push us to get up in the dark and head for the water.

Dream Fishing

J. DREW LANHAM

The drive from our house in Edgefield County, South Carolina, to the little fishing hole at Cheves Creek was a short one—maybe a quarter of a mile up the dirt track to the west, and then maybe a mile or two on the blacktop, and a half mile or so down the gravelly Forest Service Road. Cheves Creek—we always called it "Shaver's Creek"—is an aquatic branch of the watershed that nourishes Steven's Creek, that feeds the Savannah River, which is consumed some 125 miles southeast-downstream by the brackish Tybee Roads estuary, that spills all its upstream self into the Atlantic Ocean. I've heard since I grew up and moved away that our home place creek was named for a free black man in the mid-1800s. I've never been able to confirm that, but it gives me a special connection to the creek that makes it even more meaningful because of who we were: a black, land-owning, farming family. Black mostly hasn't been the favored color in Edgefield County, home of a slew of racist governors, including Strom Thurmond and "Pitchfork" Ben Tillman.

I didn't know any of this history, good or bad, as a kid growing up in the mid-1970s. What I did know was that, besides the rain puddles and ditches where I used to play-fish, it was the only water big enough to hold my imagination. At ten years old, I wasn't concerned with the source of Cheves Creek, nor its destination. I did know, though, that unlike the ephemeral places where I hoped some imaginary bass would magically take a wormless, hookless string tied to a broken branch, there were fish in Cheves Creek for sure. Although a short portion of it brushed against our property line down in the bottom, we had to venture onto the "gub'ment" land a few miles away for the best—and real-est fishing.

On some summer afternoons there were clear signs that wetting a hook was more important than whatever endless list of home place tasks needed doing. With the katydids clocking in to the evening shift and the cows grazing in the pasture, procrastination became the priority. We put off chores for later. The essential task was suddenly a trip to the fishin' hole. There were clues. Sometimes it was obvious, like Daddy digging a Crisco can full of wriggling, red worms out of the shit-full feedlot. Sometimes the serious work of the day—oiling some rusty iron thing or plowing some dusty, weedy place—degraded into dawdling. Reorganizing the tackle box, sorting through rainbow tangles of jellied plastic worms, and taming the hook-toothed hordes of brightly colored lures were an almost certain sign. The day's fate was sealed if Daddy lashed the cane poles to the side of the truck and called on us to load up. Once we were all doused with enough bug spray to choke the mosquitoes before they got anywhere close, it was time to go. Mama rode shotgun in the '49 Ford, and the rest of us piled into the truck bed. As the old truck sped up the dirt road, we sat on the tailgate and let our feet dangle downward, bouncing off the ground as responsibility faded in a cloud of dust.

The woods we entered on that creek-bound road were tall, dark, and deep. Loblollies on the ridges gave way downhill to towering tulip poplars and monstrous sweetgums in the flats that only let pieces of sky peek through. The water was hidden from sight, but its presence was palpable. The metallic odor of freshwater and fish melded into the greasy green vapor of July humidity. The scent hung heavily and pleasantly. If the rains had come within the last day or two, the water rushing through the shallow channel roared loudly as if eager to be something bigger. And then there it was: just ahead where the road punched a hole through the forest, Cheves Creek. The closer we approached, the louder the rushing roar became. It spilled like warm molasses and sometimes two feet deep over the cement crossing. Daddy parked the truck short of the ford and we piled out, untangling poles and lines in anticipation of what lay beneath the dark flow. First things first, though—the black hole below the falls where all the fish waited to get caught was on the other side of the flooded crossing. The creek may as well have been the Red Sea to us kids, and there was no Moses with a magical staff to part the path. There was only Daddy.

The crossing was more often under the water than above it. Upstream, Cheves Creek ran broad and smooth. It looked deceptively peaceful pouring over the concrete pad. Daddy knew better, though, and hardly ever drove across it, fearing the powerful flow would sweep the truck away. The footing was dangerous at best, the slab snotty-slick with green algae. Daddy wouldn't let any of us cross it by ourselves. He feared that we'd fall into the current. He was even more afraid of a drainpipe whirl-pool on the upstream side that drew leaves, sticks, and everything else down into an abysmal drainpipe. It terrified everybody except my older brother Jock, who would stand dangerously close to the death-well, which made a terrible sucking sound. He'd throw things down its maw just to marvel in the power of the hydraulic. My brother was like that, always daring life to see what more could be pulled from it.

Daddy didn't tempt fate the way my brother did. He wrestled it to the ground and held it there until it did his bidding. At times he was more god than man to me. He'd take the poles, bait, and other tackle over first by himself and then, like a big, brown, broad-shouldered ferry, return for each of us, holding our hands to steady us on the slippery trip across the slick pad. Fishing was the only time I remember holding Daddy's hand. His swallowed mine. The calluses from all that wood-splitting, nail-hammering, and tractor-driving gripped my palm like a vise; his fingers wrapped around mine like steel bands. My faith in that grasp was complete. Physical contact in my family was a rare thing. No one ever said "I love you." In those moments of closeness it was unspoken, acted out. Deep down it meant everything.

Once safely across, more warnings came. Time spent around water back then brought cautionary tales from Mama and Daddy about the dangerous cottonmouth moccasins that lurked around the fishing hole. Sure, there was the occasional snake slithering off a log, disturbed by our intrusion, or the rare bold water snake that tried to steal a fish from the live-stringer, but in all my time wandering about in places where cottonmouths should've been, I never saw one—not a single one. Country folk tell all kinds of tales about snakes. There are coach-whips swallowing their own tails to roll like wheels in pursuit of unlucky people who they'd beat with their tails once subdued; demon-possessed rattle-snakes re-joining and reanimating themselves after being beheaded *and* chopped in half again for good measure; and black racers chasing folks just for the hell of it. Water moccasins held their own place in snake lore though. Mean just because they could be, cottonmouths flashed tell-tale white mouths before biting the careless interloper with fangs so venomous that only heroic efforts would save their lives. The cottonmouths that we never saw may as well have been black mambas. There were tales of them being thick as a man's thigh. According to everyone in the know, a cottonmouth would not only stand its ground, but would attack with little or no provocation. Word from my grandmother, Mamatha, was that the best way to escape any snake was to run a zigzagged course as fast as possible away from the serpent. I took the warnings and the advice seriously. I'd watched enough television to want to avoid the pain of both the snake bite and the torture of cuts and poison sucking that came with it. In between climbing trees and skipping stones, I practiced this evasive technique from time to time to be sure I'd be ready when the inevitable serpent encounter occurred. I was more on alert in this wilderness than on any wandering I ever did on my own. But with the fishing just ahead, the worry was well worth it.

Finally there! We unwrapped the lines from the cane poles, adjusted the cork bobbers, slipped a sacrificial wriggling worm on the hook, and with a swing or two dropped the bait into a spot where the foam swirled just under a huge fallen log that spanned the creek. Daddy was a fishing master. Although he usually used a cane pole, he'd have other lines in the water too. If he was really serious, he'd put a live minnow on his line or maybe try one of the lures on the rod and reel. He could cast to the other side of the creek, under the log or even over it to get to the fish that were out of reach of the rank amateurs. In spite of the gigantic biting horseflies that seemed more attracted to the bug dope than repelled by it, and the occasional mirage that turned a crooked stick into an attacking cottonmouth, I was at peace beyond calm. I wanted to stay creek-side forever.

Fishing was how Daddy escaped, how he played. Sometimes he went on longer fishing expeditions without us to the big water—Clarks Hill, a hydro-electric lake holding back miles of creeks and rivers to deliver cheaper power to the people downstream. The lake's name has since been changed to Thurmond, but I refuse to give the old racist Edgefield governor that kind of respect. It taints an otherwise good memory. Daddy's trips to Clarks Hill meant at least a half day working on his old outboard motor and making sure the aluminum skiff was mostly leak free. Those expeditions were sometimes solitary trips, but on some of them one of his close friends like Cousin Monroe or Joe Frank would go along. They'd often return with few, if any, fish. I'm not sure that catching was always the mission. On a few occasions, Daddy and I would head off by ourselves to Lick Fork, a little lake a few miles from the home place— east instead of west, where I learned to swim with the catfish, bream, and bass that patrolled the murky water. When we fished together like this—just the two of us—there were never many words. They weren't necessary. It was solid deep time. I felt worthier as a son just being in his orbit. It didn't matter whether the fish bit or not. Sometimes a channel cat would take the bait, a ball of worms sitting in the mud. What seemed like a whale tugging on the other end of the line would eventually surface to reveal a grunting, whiskered ugly thing that would cook up pretty and golden-brown. "Just right for good eatin'"—was what Daddy might say.

On a good day at the Cheves Creek fishing hole, the bobbers would hit the water and within a minute or two there was a twitch, then another. If the thing underwater was worth its weight in cornmeal and hot grease, the bobber would disappear like a torpedo into the depths, taking a foot or two of stiffening line with it. On the other end, I could feel the strength of whatever it was that had sucked in the unlucky worm. Pulling back, but not too hard, the cane curved with the catch and the line would dance in the water for a few seconds as the slab of muscle struggling to stay under flashed like quicksilver back and forth. With a tug or two, and more than a few whoops and hollers, a hand-sized bream hung flipping and wriggling at the other end of the line.

Daddy often wasn't satisfied with little fish and wandered down the creek to find a hole where bigger things lurked. If he was lucky, a worm-hungry warmouth might be tempted to bite from one of the deeper holes undercutting the bank. The first pike that I ever saw was almost a foot long with a toothy, Mona Lisa grin that made it look like a miniature barracuda. Daddy held it up like it was some trophy and we all marveled at the odd fish that seemed to come only to his line.

As the stringer grew heavier and the insect repellent wore thin, it was time to surrender the evening to the night shift. Flitting bats and choruses of toads and whip-poor-wills soon overtook vireo song. The grown folks said the cottonmouths would come out soon. It was time to go. There was a mess of bream to clean. Procrastination had worn off, and there was feeding the cows and other farm work to do. A fresh-caught fried fish meal with collard greens and fresh creamed corn were added incentive to get back home and get the chores done. The fishing hole would belong to the frogs again as the day faded away.

Paducah '80
J. TODD SCOTT

'm twenty-nine years old in Los Angeles, watching the same beat-up old apartment door for hours. The car smells like Tommy's Hamburgers and my partner's Camels. He's an old-school Monterey Park detective and he's got the window open wide, and since I'm the junior guy watching the door, he gets to do nothing but watch cigarette smoke drift in the late afternoon sun, the sky red and orange and striped with con-trails over LAX.

He flips through a newspaper he's read a hundred times already.

We're waiting for a Colombian with a bad haircut and worse skin and two kilos of coke to open that door. The Colombian's supposed to drive it to Indio or Vegas or Phoenix.

My partner flicks ash, watches me over gold-rimmed readers. "Just like fishing, right?"

"What's like fishing?"

My partner has a thousand stories. He talks endlessly about his time working vice, working homicide. His stories are dark and funny and dirty—most I can't repeat to my parents or my wife—and although I've heard them all at least three times, they still make me laugh. But he hasn't spoken to me in an hour, maybe more, and his question catches me off guard, fired from an unexpected angle.

"This." He waves expansively at the Oldsmobile we're living in, the city outside the windows. That damn door I've been watching. "It's all about patience, mi amigo, a test of wills."

"I guess," I say. I'm sweating through my eyes, and although I don't smoke, I've swallowed two packs' worth just sitting in this car.

"Ahh, that's what I thought," he says. "You're from Alabama, right?"

"Kentucky," I say, "but close enough." And it is. He's never been east of Riverside. "What about you, you like fishing?"

It's not a dumb question. We're only ten miles from the ocean. I rent a place right on the sand in Playa Del Rey, no bigger and not much nicer than our Oldsmobile, but I can count the boats heading out to Catalina.

I wake mornings to the sound of fog horns; the rough grit of salt and sand on everything.

But he laughs, shaking out the newspaper for the fourth or fifth or thousandth time. I feel another story coming on.

There's always another story.

He adjusts his readers, and the blued steel thirty-eight revolver tucked in his lap.

"Me? No, I don't know anything about that country redneck stuff. Nada, amigo. I grew up in El Monte..."

There's a picture of me—

I'm nine-years-old in Paducah, Kentucky, holding a heavy catfish on line. I'm sun-dappled, standing in the long-limbed shadows of a pin oak. The fish shines quicksilver and it's just about the biggest thing in the photo.

It's trapped there, motionless; forever trying to get free.

That image stuck with me so much I used it years later in a novel, and I've used variations of it again and again. I don't know why that picture speaks to me. But that's what writers do more than we ever care to admit—tuck away old photographs of ourselves in our books and stories.

I was born in Paducah, but raised in Louisville—rural spit, suburban polish. My young parents eventually traded their singlewide parked between the barn and my grandparents' house for a two-story brick with fresh-cut lawns and rolling sprinklers.

My country roots are thin, clinging to loose soil; I left Paducah with the accent but few of the affects and none of the skills.

I didn't learn to track or hunt or skin or scale from my grandfather's knee, although I read plenty about all that stuff. I grew up mostly an "inside kid;" I liked dragons and dungeons and books about gunfighters and outlaws and faraway places. Adventures and monsters.

I spun fantastic stories and tales to myself.

For as far back as I can remember, my parents and I returned to Paducah for the holidays—small trips, usually no more than a couple of days. But when I was around twelve or so, they booked me on an extended solo bus trip "down to the farm," a summer getaway that both excited and terrified me. My grandfather, Maurice, was a mail carrier for many years, and fancied himself something of a gentleman farmer. He owned several acres in McCracken County, with a real red barn and a horse and peach and apple orchards and a grape arbor and three muddy brown ponds, all anchored by a ramshackle house. The "gentleman" part was a tennis court (unusual for the time and place) he'd grated out next to the barn—one end was the barn's western red wall. My father was a good player, and the sound of bright green balls bouncing off the weathered wood was as heavy as a heartbeat.

In truth, I'd always been leery of the farm. *That house*. It sat at odd angles and nothing seemed to fit quite right; weeds grew thick and tall along its flanks, and the wood was warped and the windowpanes hazy. Monstrous trees shadowed it. It wasn't particularly large, but felt bigger inside than out, whispering to itself with the sound of mice or rats or bats. It was at its best in the morning, filled with the smells of bacon and coffee and my grandmother Modelle's buckwheat pancakes. It was at its worst at night, when the boards moved and moaned, when the surrounding rural darkness held it tight like a fist.

There's a different dark out in the country. The houses are spread far apart, and the warm glow of windows is few and far between, and the stars are bright and clear but do little to light the way, all that empty space is somehow claustrophobic.

I had a hell of an imagination even then.

There was a room in that old house I did love, though. The roof cut an impossible, razor-sharp angle, taller on one end than the other, and it was always too hot or too cold. The wood stove did little to change that, and its ruddy glow did even less to light it. I worried about spiders weaving spires in the dark corners, feared the chilly touch of Confederate ghosts. But one wall was nothing but books—ranging wildly in genre and era, from the *Old West* and *Mysteries of the Unknown* series by

Time-Life, to Horatio Hornblower and Tom Swift and the Hardy Boys. I discovered Robert E. Howard and Edgar Rice Burroughs and my first Louis L'Amour and Zane Grey novels there, as well as H.A. DeRosso pulp westerns. Agatha Christie and Len Deighton and Maclean and McBain. My entire family loved books, and I read far and wide for my age. All the times I'd visited the farm before, my favorite thing to do was load up an armful and disappear.

That summer, without my parents and no kid my age around and no one else but all those books to keep me company, I planned to disappear a lot—inside the house, deep inside my own head.

My grandfather picked me up from the bus stop in his old brown Ford truck with the bench seats, the ones that year-round smelled like sun and hot plastic and horsehair. We rolled back to the farm with the windows down, late light turning the windshield gold; stray bits of hay and grass blowing in my face.

Paducah in August is beautiful in its own way. Hot and humid and green, the air thick with mosquitos and gnats. The farm sat at a four-way crossroads surrounded by pastures and orchards and scattered trees— Black cherry and blue ash; Sourwood and sugar hackberry and sweet birch.

The whole world sunlight and shadows.

But I ignored all that, loaded down with my own books. Old favorites *The Lord of the Rings* and *Watership Down*, and newer reads—*The Dead Zone* and Zelazny's *Roadmarks*. I still had an old *Swamp Thing* comic book curled in my hand from the long bus ride.

I'd been idly leafing through it a third or fourth time while we drove.

"So, you like them kinds of funny books?" my grandfather finally asked, rubbing old hands together, motioning at my comic and my heavy backpack. Of course, he already *knew* I did. Anyone who'd mail-ordered the entire *Mysteries of the Unknown* series sure couldn't criticize my reading tastes. As he waved dismissively at my comic, I tried to imagine just how many letters had passed through those veined hands, all the secrets and confessions and mysteries they'd contained.

"Monsters and things like that?" he continued, with a short laugh. He didn't really laugh much. "Well, son, there's nothing funny about the one we got right here."

It wasn't quite Swamp Thing, or one of the Ringwraiths, but it was close.

He called it Wampus, a great bullhead catfish—a mud cat, a mud pout—that had prowled the small pond behind the barn for years. Decades, if he was to be believed. He claimed it had developed a taste for errant tennis balls and had swallowed twice its weight worth. Many had tried to catch Wampus. All had failed.

I'd fished that pond before, catching my fair share of bluegill and crappie, slick and shiny and most no bigger than my hand, even with my fingers spread wide. The catfish from my picture had been pulled from that same muddy water, and although it was a fair specimen too, it was no behemoth. No legendary Wampus. *No monster*. In fact, such a creature had never been spoken of before. Not until that drive in that sunbaked truck.

Now, I was young and impressionable and loved to daydream, but I wasn't a complete fool, sensing the way only kids' can when an adult has ulterior motives. My grandfather's fish story had the dreaded ring of a *lesson*, and school was already out for the summer. But I was intrigued as well, already predisposed to believe in Middle Earth and monsters. And I had several long, lonely weeks ahead of me.

So, we struck a bargain. If I helped the older folks stopping by the orchard for u-pick peach bushels, he would give me the time and tools to hunt Wampus. Hell, he'd even throw in a buck for each day's work, so I could buy more of them "funny books" or whatever else I wanted.

I didn't understand then what I was agreeing to, what Faustian bargain I'd made.

But I found out as soon as the next sunrise and shrill alarm clock.

A peach orchard in the high blaze of summer is a hard place: a rural gulag.

Conan's Wheel of Pain.

An exaggeration? Maybe. But not to twelve-year-old me. I spent lifetimes up on a ladder, picking just the right fruit. The fuzz stuck to my hands and my face and inched its way like a living thing down the back of my shirt. The heat turned my arms and legs red, and that first week was like working under glass, the sun magnified into an unforgiving white light. Sauron's unblinking eye. I sweated peach juice and trailed flies. I was John Carter marooned on red Barsoom.

I earned my grandfather's dollars as I baked and browned.

But at the end of each day, as the sun mercifully wheeled down, I had the time to start my exploratory missions into Wampus's lair, the largest pond behind the barn.

My first forays were simple—a Zebco rod and reel and night crawlers and mealworms. Angling for catfish isn't hard. They're always hungry and not particularly canny. Bigger ones eat small fish, and smaller ones eat just about anything. Muscular and angry, mud cats don't have scales, just slick, slimy skin, and they can poison you with stingers on their fins. They put up a helluva good fight trying to throw a hook. There's plenty of ancient lore on the best way to catch them, as complex and contradictory as any fantasy epic. But my Wampus soon proved to be one-of-a-kind. Elusive. I worked my way through the crawlers and minnows and chicken livers and different stink baits, before getting truly exotic—canned dog food (Alpo), Big League chew, soap (Zest), Spam, and WD-40 sprayed onto chunks of hotdogs.

Even old tennis balls slathered in blood.

Frustrated, I compiled an arsenal of other weapons, including a shovel and a hoe. A length of bicycle chain. A frog-gigging stick and the metal top of a lost trashcan (a shield, perhaps).

My grandfather let me strap on his old Ruger Single Six .22, and during my orchard work-release program, I became Grey's Lassiter or L'Amour's Hondo, practicing trick shots and aiming at the sky and my reflection in the still surface of the pond.

I fished endlessly, trolling the depths for Wampus. I worked dusk and dawn, rolling out extra early before my other chores. I caught buckets of bluegill and some smaller mud cats and threw them all back. And in those quiet hours alone that a rod and reel can give you, even an old rusty Zebco, I really started to take notice of the farm itself, the pastures and fields and *life* all around me:

I cheered on red-winged blackbirds playing touch-and-go off the pond's surface, turning gyres in slants of late-afternoon sunlight.

Watched dragonflies hover near motionless in cattails, and bullfrogs slipping and sliding in the green mire.

Caught sight of a small deer eyeing me from the shadows of an apple tree.

Fired shots at a fat, bustling groundhog (I missed, but something I still regret).

Chased a bright blaze of red I would have sworn was a fox.

Counted endless, widening circles across that murky pond water.

For someone who'd spent most of his life behind walls only reading about fantasy worlds, I found myself outside all the time, drawn not just by the myth of the monster fish, but the real world beyond the window.

At night, exhausted, I'd sit with my grandfather beneath the sourwoods and watch fireflies and tell him about all the things I'd seen and done, and we'd share some fresh peach ice cream he'd hand-churned and talk about the books we were reading. The night didn't seem as scary then, that rural dark not quite as foreboding. He was a deacon at the Mt. Zion Baptist Church up the road, and sometimes when he was working on a sermon, he would ask my opinion about just the right turn of a phrase.

I was pretty good with words even then, and that ice cream was so damn good, so perfect, I didn't mind chasing it with a little hellfire and brimstone.

That summer passed as all summers do when you're young—way too fast; in the blink of an eye—and I was only a day removed from my return bus ride to Louisville when I got up before the sun.

I didn't need an alarm anymore.

The face in my bathroom mirror was thinner, tauter, feral. My skin as dark as the muddy pond itself.

I strapped on my Ruger and hauled my Zebco and my shovel and chain down to the water. I passed through the quiet barn, surrounded by old, sunburned hay, which to this day smells like nothing else. Like time passing, like summers gone by, way too fast. I stopped long enough to let my grandfather's horse nuzzle me. With all my wanderings back and forth to the pond, we'd become fast friends by then, and as I left the barn behind, I eyed purple clouds crouched low in the dawn sky, threatening rain—the only rain I can remember from that summer.

Mist hung knee-high, but the pond, as always, was immutable, unchanged.

For weeks I'd circled the monster's demesne. I'd gotten to know its moods and its colors and the rise and fall of its banks; the snake holes and slippery places. The water's edge and the nearby apple trees. Where wild blackberries ran along the fence line and the strawberry patch was thickest on the other side. The abandoned John Deere that was mostly weeds and rust. The trees and tall grass and all the shadowed, quiet resting places.

If that farm was my Middle Earth, I'd explored it all.

I'd long given up the thought of catching Wampus. The creature, if it existed at all, had evaded me like so many myths and legends do, but I'd already figured out that summer's real lesson—all those weeks running far afield, the hours in the peach orchard and the days standing quiet on the pond's bank, waiting and watching the sky and shadows and water.

Sometimes it's about the ones you don't catch. Or maybe, even empty-handed, I'd somehow caught something greater.

Either way, it had been a hell of a summer, a hell of a story. And every story, even a fish tale, needs a great ending:

The dawn sun fought the coming clouds and the wind moved the grass like breath and I was ready to go back in for breakfast when I finally saw it.

Him.

A great mud cat; colossal. Just below the surface and big enough it was visible beneath the murky water. Antediluvian. Chthonic. Pale, mottled. Roiling like smoke as thick as my waist.

Wampus lolled in the shallows, unconcerned and fearless, as all my plans and schemes and traps fell apart in its wake.

There was moss on his great back, like ancient filigree. Once green, blackened by age.

Old hooks studded his thick hide like harpoons.

He swam so sluggish he barely moved. Time itself barely moved. Slow enough for me to bait the Zebco, more than enough to take some unsteady shots with the Ruger. If I dared, I could've waded into the water after him, grabbed him up in my arms and dragged his bulk up onto the bank. Armed with my trashcan lid shield and shovel, I could have fought him in the mud like St. George and the Dragon.

But I did none of those things. Stunned, amazed, I simply watched. Just as I had with the blackbirds and dragonflies and bullfrogs. The sky and shadows and water. Minutes, hours. I couldn't say then, and still couldn't now.

The dawn sun fought the coming clouds and the wind moved the grass like breath...

I watched until Wampus headed into deeper water. Until he was a shadow and then the hint of a shadow and then nothing but a circle on the water that disappeared too.

I watched until thunder rolled in the distance, urging me on.

Then I gathered up my arms and armor and went to get some buckwheat pancakes.

The rain held off, and later that afternoon, as I was leaning against a ladder eating a raw peach, the last for me that summer, a man approached to pick a bushel. I'd seen him up at Mt. Zion during my grandfather's sermons, and knew he had a place not far from the farm. He was tall, thin, graying hair held back with some thick pomade. He was friendly, knew all about the McCracken County Scotts, so we talked about the summer heat and that morning's weird weather and peaches and sermons. He asked me about my folks in Louisville, and eventually let on that he was a federal agent, or used to be. He'd recently retired from the FBI and returned home to Paducah—to his daddy's old place, just like ours. He'd missed it, and was glad to be back.

He said you never really recognize the things that truly matter the first time around. No different than seeing someone's face you should know, but can't quite put a name to.

Going home again can be like finally remembering that name.

He told me I'd know what he was talking about, one day.

Honestly, though, I ignored all that—it sounded too much like *another* lesson. But I was fascinated by the idea of the FBI. Inspired by all those books I'd read, I pressed him on what it was like to carry a badge and a gun, to really chase bad guys and outlaws. I wanted *stories*, and he admitted it was about as fine an adventure as a man could have. You had to be smart and strong and brave. Needed a keen eye, a quick mind, and steady hand.

"Just like Lassiter," I said. "Like Hondo. Like Aragorn."

He smiled sadly, and said, "Just like that."

My grandfather died in 1994.

It was the only time I ever saw my father cry.

There was no reason for any of us to move back to Paducah then, so the farm was sold off in pieces—the house and the barn and the tennis court. The orchards and the ponds.

Wampus was sold right along with it, or so I want to believe.

My grandmother spent her remaining years in a nursing home, and when we used to visit, I'd try to talk about summers and buckwheat pancakes and peaches, but she didn't seem to remember those things. Not the way I did. She passed away in 2006.

She was buried next to my grandfather in Mt. Zion Cemetery, right behind the church.

I went to college in Virginia, majored in English, and enrolled in a lot of creative writing and literature courses; even thought I might become a famous science fiction or fantasy author. Or maybe the next Stephen King or Larry McMurtry. I wrote lots of stories; a half-dozen half-finished novels full of swordsmen and gunfighters. Heroes and sorcerers and cowboys and outlaws. More than a few monsters. But I never quite forgot that conversation in the orchard, either. That retired agent, who took the time to share a peach and a talk with me, made a point of stopping by grandfather's house later that same day and dropping off an old fingerprint kit and some evidence bags and even a replica badge.

With my grandfather's Ruger on my hip and that plastic badge on my belt, I really felt like Lassiter.

That agent, whose name I can't remember, died from pancreatic cancer before the next summer.

My senior year, just before graduation, I put aside all my stories and applied to be a federal agent through DEA's Louisville District Office. Although it took a while to get on (long enough that I went to law school in the interim), I finally entered the DEA academy in Quantico, Virginia in 1995.

Fifteen years after that one long, memorable Paducah summer.

Later that same year, I transferred to my first post—Los Angeles.

I'm twenty-nine years old in Los Angeles, watching the same beat-up old apartment door for hours…we're waiting for a young Colombian with a bad haircut and worse skin and two kilos of coke to open that door…

We didn't catch that Colombian that day, or any day after. I've been an agent now for more than two decades, and learned long ago it happens that way, more often than not.

That's okay. It's just the job. Like the late nights and never-ending reports or sitting in a car for hours, staring at the same damn door.

It's all about patience, a test of wills.

Endless time…where you do nothing but wait and watch the sky and the shadows and the water; where you and your partner talk about your lives and your problems and swap endless jokes and stories. The same ones over again, forever refining and revisiting. And that's the other thing I've learned—agents and cops are damn good storytellers. Some of the best.

I never fished much after that Paducah summer. I moved seven times, all over the world. And with the farm gone, it just never quite felt the same.

Again, that's okay. It's just life.

I haven't gone home again, either. Not yet.

But after all the years gone by, I did start writing again.

There are these things I remember, as real as any photograph, although no picture still exists. They're tucked away in every book I write, and always will be—

The grit of peach fuzz on sunburned skin.

The clack of an old ice cream churner; the crunch of ice and salt and sweet peach ice cream on my lips.

The rough touch and smell of an old paperback book.

The hard sharpness of a metal fishhook.

The heat of a setting sun, sweat beaded on my face.

The cool of the water and the hum and the buzz of bugs.

The wick and whisper of cattails against my knees.

The dawn sun and the moving clouds and the wind moving the grass like breath…

Some Crazy Sh*t
FRANK BILL

I t was the two-man boat from my mother in-law—made of weathered-aluminum, worn-fiberglass with rusted holes where screws were missing along seams, a broken vinyl seat not meant for a person with questionable balance—that worried me at the start.

I didn't wanna fucking sink. Or fall out and drown.

Only having an oar and a pocketknife as a weapon would weigh on me later. No one could've predicted what would happen before the first braided, 20lb test Spider Wire fishing line hit Indian Creek.

Going back, I can't remember if we'd planned on fishing that day or if my brother-in-law, Israel, with his salt and pepper hair he kept high and tight, a partial sleeve tattoo, always a swell of chew in his lip, had phoned me out of the blue asking if I'd wanted to go. What I do recall was his driving a black, corroded 2001 Nissan Frontier 4x4 he'd found in a local ad. He'd paid a visit to the owner and bought the truck without consulting my sister-in-law, Gayle. When he drove home, she was pissed. "That's a piece of shit!" were her exact words.

In that truck, we headed out of Corydon, Indiana with four treadless-tires, a front end out of whack, an undercarriage that looked to have been kept in saltwater, and a two-man boat from my mother-in-law. Coming with a camp she'd recently purchased, the boat had been upside down on the patched grass and dirt hillside of the yard just waiting to go fishing or sink us. Israel hadn't checked to make sure it would even float. He just strong-manned it into the bed of the Nissan, picked me and my tackle up, and off we went a few miles from his place on Big Indian Road back behind a dam on Indian Creek.

Surrounded by the vegetation of farming pastures, woods, and the rustling sound of the interstate off in the distance, we pulled off the side of the busted road where signs posted NO PARKING. We parked.

Stepping from the truck in my cut-off khakis, t-shirt and worn-Keens, a medium sized black Lab pup came from nowhere, tongue lapping its jaws with a panted-rush of excitement like a hyper child needing Ritalin, demanding our attention.

After patting the dog, we made sure our bait, tackle, rods, reels, and two oars were in the boat. The crazed canine pup with its salivating tongue circled us with frantic energy as we carried everything down the steep-rocky-hillside of weeds and mud to a flat area of moist soil, emerald foliage, vine and briar where rabbit would burrow around the creek. Scents were of fishy water. Molded timber and countryside. The creek was a glassy darkness of movement.

The place to our far left, where the stream rolled over the dam and crashed down, worried me some. You had to make sure you didn't get stuck in the current once your boat was in the water. You had to make sure you traveled against it so you didn't get swept over the dam.

Fishing here in the past, I'd taken home many ivory-bellied bass, double-jumbo-biscuit sized crappie, and bluegill so black-light-glowing blue it'd make pro fisherman froth at the mouth.

Once, hitting the creek from dusk to dawn with my nephew, we reeled in bass and bluegill, emptying all of the deep honey holes. We filled a crappie basket and lined my stringer with our catch. Dark came, and calling it a day, I still remember what I believe were bass jumping and splashing about the creek's surface as my nephew navigated us to the weeded shoreline with the trolling motor. For twelve hours of fishing, the crappie basket had stayed connected to the side of our boat, its easy open lid worn out, resting in the water all day, holding its shape in the deep areas we'd fished. But getting out of the boat, water sloshing over my Keen sandals, my feet sinking and sliding, me pushing and my nephew pulling, the basket's lid opened. Over half our days catch swam away.

My stringer was good. My temperament not so much. Pissed off is one way of summing up that moment.

Now, wrestling the weight of the boat through the weeds with the Lab irritating us like a mosquito, we got the boat half way in the water. Looking at Israel, I said, "I'm not getting in unless I know it won't sink."

His assurance: "It won't sink."

"You go out in it first."

"Fine. I will." And he did.

We didn't have life jackets. Each of us could swim. Not that accidents couldn't happen. I'd heard plenty of fishing stories over the years about guys fishing close to a dam, capsizing their boats, and getting pulled under to their deaths.

Israel pushed off from the weedy shore with one of the oars. Got out into the deeper area some twenty feet away. I held the opposite end of a rope knotted through a metal eyehole to secure the boat's front. No water rushed in, and my safety radar was quieted.

Hand over hand, I pulled the boat in close. Wading out, I stepped in the boat then pushed away from the shore with an oar. The black Lab was still running around all harebrained and puppified, splashing out towards us. The creek deepened. The dog changed directions. Made it back to the weeded shore. Disappeared.

We situated ourselves, paddling away from the dam, moving maybe forty or fifty feet from where we launched. Grabbing our rods—I used an Ugly Stick, and I believe Israel had a Zebco—we got ready to make a quick cast to test the waters for a bite. Before we could even move upstream, a shrieking cry broke out from the weeds up on the shore, similar in sound to that of a baby goat. We stood stone-still and eyed the shore area. Then came a playful growl and a bark. Another cry, almost a whine. And more barking.

Israel looked at me. "What the fuck?"

There was nothing to be seen. Only heard.

"Sounds like a baby goat." I said.

All at once, barreling up from the weeds, came the snort and stomp of hooves behind the yelping of the black Lab. The Lab was headed for the water. Headed towards us. Dropping our rods down in the boat. Hearts pounding in our throats. We traded rods for oars. It was a deer. A large doe honing in on the Lab. Each was now treading water. The doe splashing. The Lab swimming.

Stomping down on the Lab, the doe took pleasure in making it yelp until the Lab sunk into the water. Bubbles erupted from the creek. The deer kept stomping. The Lab resurfaced a few feet away from the doe. From us. The doe followed. Still stomping. The Lab dog-paddled and sank beneath the water once more. Israel and I stood shell-shocked-quiet clenching the oars. Ready to place a beat-down on the doe.

Then time stopped. The Lab had disappeared beneath the water. No bubbles. The doe stood like a statue eyeing us, the creek lined her chest. We were immersed in a stare down with the crazed black-olive-eyed doe. Waiting for movement. A hint of action. Of what would transpire next. All at once, slow and territorial, the doe turned. Splashed through the water to the shore. Made her way to where we believed her baby lay. Then bedded down where we couldn't see because of the foliage.

"Dude? That's the craziest fucking shit I ever seen."

"No shit!"

"Where's the fuckin' dog?"

Waiting, the creek's surface was calm. We watched and watched. Then bubbles arched from the creek. The dog's head emerged from the water, way off behind us. Close to the dam. Huffing for wind. Fighting the current, the dog paddled. Swam hard to the shoreline. Made it to solid ground. Took off rocket-style-running up the embankment we'd carried the boat down. Then the road. And disappeared.

Israel looked at me.

"Thought that son of a bitch was gonna attack us."

"Me too."

"The hell you think happened?"

"Dog must've been messing with the doe's baby. Pissed it off."

Laughing, dropping his oar, "Goddamn that was some crazy shit."

And it was.

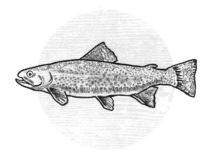

A Dream of Trout
ERIC RICKSTAD

The first time I ever fished was with my father.

I am four years old, maybe five. It is evening, and we are standing in the small brook trout tributary that spills behind our A-frame camp toward the Mad River a couple miles downstream in Fayston, Vermont. My father is standing beside me as I grip an old Eagle Claw fiberglass rod and work the closed-faced Zebco, preparing my first cast.

The past two summers, I have stood on this stream bank and watched trout fin in the water, and watched my father fish, and marveled at the brookies he's lain on the dark, wet ferns at the bottom of his wicker creel.

Already, I love trout, and I love the clear cold pure water they need to survive, and the woods and fields through which that waters slips and tumbles. Already, I dream of trout, dream of what it is like to send a worm down into a trout's world, trick one into taking the bait, and bring one from its world to mine, to feel it in my hand.

This evening, with my father, I am finally fishing instead of watching. I thumb the reel's button and bring the rod back. "Right there," my father says, "behind that rock, let the worm work down through there. They like it in there."

I cast and watch my line. It stops, and I feel a small jolt. My dad exclaims, "Set the hook. You got one." I sense that my father cannot believe what I've done on the first cast of my life, and is surprised and proud. "You're good," he says. My heart pounds as I bring the brook trout to me and kneel to take it in my hands. It is a living gem. Gorgeous. Strong. Cold. "Can we keep it?" I ask. My father says, "What do you say we leave him for seed? We won't have time to catch enough for a meal anyway."

I work the hook from its jaw and release the trout back into the stream and watch it sit there and fin in the riffle.

My mind is alive with dreams of a lifetime of fishing I'll share with my father. The wild places we'll go, the monstrous, dogged trout we will catch, a lifetime of adventures with him courses through me in that moment.

Except, soon after that evening, my father will leave me and my three sisters and our mother. I will see him now and again in later years, but we will rarely fish.

My mother, trying to raise my three sisters and me alone while working fulltime as a clerk at a hardware store hardly has time to breathe, let alone take a young son fishing. She would not know where to begin anyway.

She's never fished in her life and knows nothing of fishing. Nothing. She is indifferent to it, too, and does not understand its elemental draw that snags in one's DNA or doesn't. She has said as much.

I cannot visit, let alone fish the one trout stream I know, the one behind our A-frame. It is forty miles from our house, and we don't go there anymore. It's my father's camp now, not *ours*.

There are no trout streams near our house, not near enough for a boy as young as I to get to on his own. Still, my head swims with dreams of trout, and fishing for them in their cold streams, in the shade of woods, and of the hope my father will return to take me trout fishing.

But my father does not return. I see him once or twice, and ask to fish, but he is always too distracted and too busy, and then he is gone again.

For a couple years, I never fish.

I flip through *Field & Stream* and *Sports Afield* magazines my father has left behind, escaping into the pictorials of Labrador, Maine, and Alaska, envisioning the day I will fish these faraway waters. I practice casting in our back yard. I dig up worms in the garden and pick night crawlers at night, pack a coffee can full of them, so I am ready, just in case.

One afternoon, as I practice casting in the yard, I hear a voice behind: "Want to go fishing."

I turn to see my mom.

She is home from work.

"Dad's here!" I say, reeling up line fast.

"No," she says. "I'll take you."

"You?"

"Why not?" she says.

How will she ever take me fishing, I wonder. She knows nothing about it. Still, excitement lights in me. My mom does not have to know how to fish. If she is willing to drive me to a trout stream, I am willing to fish it.

•••

In the car, we drive in the opposite direction that we'd take to get to camp.

I am confused. I don't know any other place to trout fish except camp.

"Where are we going?" I ask.

"The LaPlatte," she says.

The LaPlatte? I think. The LaPlatte is a slow, warm stream that often runs brown from silt and clay. We drive past it all the time on the way to town. It's a ditch. If it has anything more than chubs in it, I'd be shocked.

"I asked some of the guys at work where a young fisherman like you could catch some fish. They said the LaPlatte was the place to go, and gave me a secret spot." She grips the wheel, smiles a tight smile. I've never seen her so nervous.

"The LaPlatte is warm water," I say.

My mom doesn't say anything. She doesn't know what that means.

We arrive at a parking area and take a hiking trail that leads us down to the stream. The hiking trail is rutted and rocky and muddy from being so well trod. Signs with arrows point the way. Several times, my mom slips and nearly falls in her work sneakers. I grab her and hold her upright. "Sorry," she says, though I am not sure for what she is apologizing. We manage to make it to a fishing hole where forked sticks are shoved into the banks, and empty beer cans and spent candy wrappers litter the tramped grass around fire pits.

The water is tepid and cloudy, the back eddies frothed with foam.

"Looks like a good spot," my mom says. "The guys at work should know. They said a boy could catch as many fish as he could stand to catch right here. So. Go on. Have fun. Fish."

•••

My mom sits on a stump beside the fire pit, toes a piece of broken bottle into the fire ring. This is not what I envisioned, this is not the dream, yet I set my coffee can of worms down and thread a worm on the hook and cast it out into the bubble line in the slow warm water. And get a tug straight away.

"Got one!" I shout without a thought, an instinctive reaction.

My mom stands up as I crank the reel and bring in a fat chub.

It is ugly, and its flesh is soft and slack in my hands, relative to the brook trout I caught with my father; but, it is lively.

I cast again. "Another!" I shout.

This time, I reel in a perch.

My mom stands right behind me, her hand on my back. "You're a good fisherman," she says.

For the next hour, I cast and cast, but I do catch not catch another fish. My hands are filthy with dirt from handling worms, and the webs of flesh between my fingers itches and burns from where the spiked dorsal fins of the perch speared it.

Finally, my mother says, "We have to go. I have to get dinner ready and get some clothes in the wash for you and your sisters."

On the drive home, my mother says, "Did you have a good time?"

As much fun as I had, I still dream of trout. "Yes," I manage to say.

"I'm sorry," she says, "The guys told me it was a great spot."

"It was," I say, "It was great."

In the decades since that day, I've been fortunate to fish most of the places I dreamed of fishing when I was a boy. Twice, I've flown in on de Havilland Beaver bush planes to the remote waters of Labrador, where I caught huge wild brook trout on mouse patterns and tiny dry flies. I've fished for wild brookies in the vast backwoods of Maine, for massive

rainbow trout in the heart of the Alaska wilderness, and for native cut-
throats a day's hike into the backcountry of Montana and Wyoming.

I have a daughter now, and a son. She is seven. He is two.

They have both taken to fishing as I did. They both have that gene, or
the bug, or the DNA, or whatever we anglers wish to call it. My daughter
caught her first fish when she was three, on a worm, cast from her pink
fiberglass rod, and reeled in with a closed-face reel. A pumpkinseed.
She loves to fish for brook trout with me on our local secret brook trout
stream, and enjoy a streamside lunch on a tiny gravel bar. Her brother
joins us on the tiny, slow warm water creek I can see from my window
now as I write this and the snow falls on this December day decades
removed from that day my mother took me fishing.

Each of the past five springs, my daughter asks if the little creek next
door, with nothing in it but chubs and black-nosed dace, is fishable.
Each spring I try to explain, "Not yet, in a few more weeks," and she
insists we go try it anyway, because "You never know when they might
bite. They could start biting today."

So, we dig up some worms and we grab her rod and reel, and we grab
her little brother who is already begging for his own rod, and who daps
at the water with a stick and shouts, "I got one, too. I got one too!"

While fishing for chubs and dace with my kids, I think of what my
mother did for me that day, her not knowing a thing about fishing, but
bothering to ask the guys at the hardware store on my behalf, and ven-
turing out to do something she had never done before, slipping on the
rocks and in the mud, and unable to help me in any way except to bring
me to the spot and be there for me. And I think, if I had to make a choice
between that one day of fishing with my mom and every other day I've
spent fishing in all those far flung places I'd dreamt of for so many years,

I'd take that one hour with my mom, each and every time, the reality of my mom's love that day far outweighing any dream a boy might have.

For My Father
WILLIAM BOYLE

Growing up, I didn't give a shit about fishing. Fishing was for kids with fathers. I didn't have one, a father. He'd split on me and my mom, left us in our small ground floor apartment in Brooklyn while he started a new family in Jersey, in a town three bridges away. He had two new sons. I imagined he took them fishing every weekend.

Beyond that, I didn't think of fishing as something you could do in the city. Fishing was for upstate. It was for the country. You needed woods, a river that wasn't murder, the right clothes, a pole, a certain frame of mind. You couldn't be the kind of kid who hyperventilated when he was too far away from concrete.

Fishing seemed peaceful. Somewhere, a father was clutching his son's shoulder, teaching him to cast off, teaching him to listen and watch, telling him stories about going fishing with his old man and his old man going fishing with his old man, all these smiling men happily bonded through history over this common love. That's what I thought.

Fishing wasn't me.

I was happy with my books and cassette tapes in my quiet little room. I liked renting movies.

Gravesend Bay wasn't far from our apartment. Just a few blocks. I'd sometimes go there and watch the light hit the surface of the water, the big cruise ships passing under the Verrazano. This wasn't water I thought people could fish from. Rats scurried on the sludgy rocks. Drunks chucked cans as far out as they could. The Belt Parkway thrummed by.

I asked my grandpa about fishing one day. He was a mechanic and fix-it guy. He spent his time under hoods and digging around in the guts of those big old TVs people don't have anymore. He had a basement full of car parts and picture tubes, antennas and old jazz 78s. I wanted to know if he'd ever gone fishing.

"Shit, sure," he said. "Me and your Uncle Whitey used to go fishing now and again."

Whitey wasn't my uncle. He was my grandfather's friend or cousin; I was never quite sure.

"Whitey used to get bombed and fall out of the boat," my grandfather continued. "Harry the Horse had a pole once, but I think he lost it playing craps."

I forgot all about fishing after that. Until college.

I went to a small state school in the Hudson Valley in a town called New Paltz, about eighty miles from the city. The leaves exploded with colors I'd never seen that first fall. I made friends, and we went on long walks through the woods. I read John Burroughs and Walt Whitman. I tried not to be scared of the dark. I tried to listen to the sounds the trees made. I tried these things with and without drugs.

I thought I should know the things I didn't know.

Fishing was one.

I bought a cheap pole at a sporting goods store, some line and hooks and bait. The guy tried to sell me a tackle box, and I shook him off.

I bought a flannel shirt and some decent boots and a pair of dark jeans at the Salvation Army.

I bought a soft pack of Lucky Strikes at the beer distributor, and I kept them in the breast pocket of the shirt with a book of matches.

I bought a twelve-pack of Yuengling there, too.

I had no money left.

I didn't know what to do with the pole. I didn't know where to start. I didn't even know about getting a permit. I could've asked one of my friends for help, but I didn't want them to think I was dumb. I just wanted to walk into the woods and find a fishing hole and come out an ace fisherman. I'd tell stories about it forever. I'd teach others to fish.

New Paltz is right at the base of the Shawangunk Ridge. The Wallkill River passes through the heart of the village. I had no shortage of places I could go.

I found a quiet spot right off the Wallkill Valley Rail Trail. A concrete bunker covered in graffiti on the wooded banks of the river served as my home base. Broken bottles and condom wrappers littered the ground. A sleeping bag had been gutted of its fluff in the corner. I settled down and opened a beer and tried to make sense of the pole. I got a hook out.

I thought of my father and his other sons.

I thought of the fish in the river. I didn't know what I'd do if I caught one. I guessed I'd just put it in the box with the cold beer and bring it home and fry it in a pan. People just cooked fish whole, right?

I lit a cigarette. It seemed true that cigarettes and beer were better when you were fishing.

But I wasn't fishing yet. I couldn't call my mission successful until

I'd dangled some line in the water. I was sure I didn't even have the language right. Did you dangle a line? That sounded pretty bad.

I kept hoping someone would come along, an old pro who could get me started, a man or woman whose kids had gone to college in faraway states and was looking to help some sorry-ass shitheel who couldn't tell a fishhook from his mother's anxiety meds.

I drank a few more beers and smoked a few more cigarettes. Somehow, I cut my hand on the hook. A real gash across my palm. It felt symbolic. I thought about the first aid kits they'd been selling at the sporting goods store. I wished I had one. Instead, I took off the new shirt and I tried to rip the sleeves from it, but it was a well-made shirt and the sleeves wouldn't tear off, so I just wound up bunching the whole thing around my bleeding hand like some sort of weird glove.

Now I was sitting there without a shirt on. I was hairy. It was getting to be dusk.

If anyone stumbled across me at this point, I didn't know what they'd think.

I burned some of the fluff from the sleeping bag for fun. It let off a horrible smell.

I went close to the water with the pole. This wasn't some raging river. It was still and dark and sad. I tried to make the pole do what it was supposed to do. With my good hand, I had figured out how to bait the hook. Or I thought I had. Nothing seemed to be going right. I brought the pole back over my shoulder and made the motion that I had seen people make in movies, but I wound up letting go of it somehow and the pole went whooshing out into the water. It sat on the surface for a few seconds before sinking under.

I laughed.

I laughed more than I'd ever remembered laughing.

I went back to the bunker. It was really getting dark.

I drank all of the remaining beers in a marathon effort. I had something to prove. I passed out, huddled against the concrete wall.

When I woke up, it was the middle of the night and dead quiet. The river was there, but it sounded gone. I was freezing with no shirt on. My hand throbbed, and I realized I'd pissed myself.

That's my fishing story.

I'm almost forty now. I have two kids, a son and daughter. We live in Mississippi. We have woods behind our little house, deer everywhere, creeks and streams not far away. I'm still no fisherman. I have a pole, a cheap one, bought in a fever of yearning for the sacramental (probably after reading Jim Harrison). This past Christmas, my daughter asked for a "twirly dress" and a fishing pole, which about sums her up. My son also wanted a pole. Thanks to my wife, they know the woods, they're comfortable in nature. They can do things naturally that I don't seem to be made for.

That night, alone in the riverside bunker, pole gone, drunk off my ass, I remember thinking, *Fathers, this is what happens when you abandon your sons.* I probably cried. I was crying a lot in those days and it would've made perfect sense to break down crying after having a crazy laughing fit. What I didn't see then, what I couldn't see then, was the future: this wife, these kids, all accepting me for what I couldn't do and what I'd never be as much as anything else. It's easier now. That kind of love makes things easier. Maybe my kids will teach me to fish one day.

Wooly Bugger
SCOTT GOULD

I guess my old man was dreading the talk, probably as much as I was. This was the hot summer he and I worked on the place at Lake Murray—a long, sweaty process during which I learned how to tack fiberglass insulation between attic joists and stir Minwax for paneling and dig a French drain so it actually flowed in the right direction. I didn't realize it was also the summer to receive the talk about the pitfalls, upsides, and intricacies of sex. At least he took me fishing when he gave me the talk.

To be honest, I thought my old man had missed his window. I was already fifteen and had gathered some rudimentary knowledge on my own. Not to say I'd graduated, but I was a quick study and didn't mind homework. (And don't you dare roll your eyes at me being fifteen and just getting the talk. This was decades ago, before you could call up any speck of information you wanted—including helpful visual aids—with a couple of thumb-strokes on a cell phone.) Most of the guys I knew—my older friends at least—never had to squirm through the awkwardness of the talk with their fathers. They'd learned everything worth knowing from this girl named Brittany who was a couple of years ahead of me in school. She'd educated half the boys in the county. The school district should have given her a plaque or something.

One of those steamy South Carolina afternoons in August, the old man said we needed to talk about *something* and told me to pull down the five weights from the shed where we stored our tools. A foreign look crossed his face, like he was confused by a math problem he couldn't solve in his head. I tried to remember what I had done wrong and came up empty. We were in the midst of nailing in some purlins on the roof. It seemed an odd time to put the hammers down and a bad time to start fishing. It was too damn hot. Anything big would be settled down in the deeper, cooler water, so I figured we'd be trying to surprise some bream. Still, nobody with good sense fished in the heat of the day. The only thing you could catch then was a tan.

If I remember correctly, the fly rods were the first things the old man put in the shed when we finished it, almost like he'd built it just to house them. He always treated his fly rods with care, even these five weights, which were the old, dinged up bamboo rods we used for bream and small mouth, not the better ones we saved for trout fishing in the mountains. The rods spanned the shed, hanging on a couple of tenpenny nails. I grabbed the fly boxes too, although for bream you only needed a couple of menu choices.

Bream would eat just about anything you wiggled in front of them. They aren't the most discerning creatures I've ever come across.

Down at the water, the old man tugged the dented johnboat into the weeds. My mother was there that afternoon, and I remember her looking at the old man and saying, "Good luck," which should have been an obvious tell, if I'd had my radar up. My mother never wished us luck when we took off in the boat. She was a smart woman. She knew luck had nothing to do with fishing. Fishing was about a lot of things: the humidity, the cover, the water temperature, the color of the bait, the color of the water, the depth of the water, the barometric pressure, the wind direction, the time of day, the time of year, the time of the moon phase, the way you held your mouth. Things like that. If you fished a good bit, you knew luck wasn't something you carried around in your tackle box.

The old man wanted to paddle. Another tell I didn't catch. Normally, he sat me in the back of the johnboat and let me do the work. He always told me he'd had enough paddling during forestry summer camps back when he was in college. I'd heard all those forester stories more than once. About how he and his buddies were so good with chainsaws, they could drive tent stakes by dropping trees on them or how he could paddle a canoe so fast, it would plane out like a motorboat. "I'm heading for the beds," he said once we settled in the johnboat. "We need supper." We'd eaten so much bream that summer I'd started checking the underside of my jaw for gills.

"We fishing or talking?" I said as the old man worked us to the back of the cove. I knew something was up. I just didn't know what. And frankly, I didn't like to talk when I fished. It seemed irreverent. I'm still that way. And I still make up little scenes. I mean, since I was a kid, I'd been thinking of fish as possessing all the things humans enjoyed on dry land. Grocery stores and neighborhoods and elementary schools and restaurants. When I cranked my spinning rod or stripped a fly through the water, I'd imagine my lure dragging right by a local bar. One of the fish on his barstool would think, *I'd better step outside and check that out.* Call me stupid, but I figured if I made up little fish scenes and little fish places, I'd catch more big fish. In other words, when I fished, I liked to think. Not carry on a conversation.

He stopped paddling, but I seemed to be the one sweating. I mopped my face with a bandana that smelled of Minwax. "Hand me a Woolly Bugger," the old man said, ignoring my question.

I cracked open a fly box and passed him one. The Woolly Bugger is truly a renaissance fly. It works anywhere, attracts anything that swims. I'd pulled trout out of back water eddies with it. I'd caught smallmouth, largemouth, once a really confused gar. And when I drifted a Woolly Bugger through a bream bed, it was like the fish were all addicts and I had their next fix dangling on the end of my leader. But it was an ugly fly. It looked like a caterpillar with issues, fuzzy and black with a back end of exploding hackles. When my dad tied his Woolly Buggers, he liked to add a turn of flashabou in the tail. Just for fun.

In the humid air over the water, I smelled the funk of the bream beds even before he dropped the half cement block we used for an anchor. Back in the shallows, three beds stood out just under the surface, the size and shape of truck tires, outlined in white with the dark, working part of the bed in the middle of the circle. I saw some hand-sized bream cruising the outer edges of the beds, keeping watch, I guessed. I started concocting something in my head about a fish fort and fish sentries, and I reached for my rod to start rigging up a fly.

"Before we get going," the old man said and stopped. He was a smart guy. Analytical, logical, articulate. He was after *something*. I wanted to fish. I stripped a few feet of fly line out of the reel, grabbed the leader and ran my fingers down it, checking for nicks and wind knots.

"I didn't think they'd be out in this heat," I said, pointing toward the beds and the gray shadows fanning at their edges.

"You know how that bream bed works, right? You know what's going on in there?" he asked me, which seemed like odd questions. Too technical or biological or something. I like to think I cocked my head at him when he said that, like a dog deciphering a far-off whistle.

"What do you mean, work?" I said. I thought the old man was getting just like me—making up fish scenarios, this time about where bream clocked in for their jobs. Then something clicked in my brain, and I felt a little hollow spot open up in my gut. Maybe it was his strange tone of voice or the slow delivery of his words. I suddenly knew what was happening: this was the talk. This was when my father was going to throw back a curtain on the most mysterious part of the world and let me see how the levers were pulled. So to speak.

The old man had a fly rod in his hand, so I knew he couldn't help but cast while he waited for me to say something. That man could handle a fly rod. Still can, even as he's sliding down the backside of his eighties. He's one of those guys who has this effortless, instinctive rhythm you can't learn from a book or a YouTube video. Like a major leaguer who can crank a hundred mile an hour fastball and make it look as easy as opening a screen door.

He learned to fish when he got married to his Alabama bride and decided to carve out a living as a forester in the south, which when you think about it, was a relatively bold move for a Chicago boy fresh off his hitch in the Army. He and his new brother-in-law decided to take up fly fishing since they were both living a half day's drive from prime trout territory. The old man took to fly fishing like he was born for it. He learned how to rig a rod, which weight line to use, how to hand-tie leaders. He practiced like a man possessed. (More stories I've heard time and again.) It wasn't long before he could drop a Parachute Adams into a coffee can at eighty feet. He could roll cast, single haul, toss sidearm against a headwind. When a fly was on the end of his leader, it wasn't just some feathers and yarn and thread wrapped around a hook. It was a living thing. It rode the air for him like an honest-to-god bug.

He tried to pass his skills onto me when I was barely big enough to hold a rod. He tried to teach me the rhythm of the cast, how to get some momentum going when you pulled the fly line off the water, how to hesitate long enough for the loop to unfurl behind you. He taught me how to shoot the line forward at the right time, but not too hard, just enough to launch the fly ahead of you. The old man was one of those Watch-Me-And-Do-Like-I-Do teachers. He figured if I observed him long enough, I'd be able to imitate his ability. And believe me, I watched. I studied him from my perch on the banks of the Chattooga, on creeks in the Smokies, sitting on the earth dams of farm ponds in Williamsburg County. I swear I tried to make mental notes that I could summon up at will. There was really only one problem: I pretty much sucked when it came to handling a fly rod.

I was too impatient and too forceful. I wanted everything too quickly. The rod never really felt comfortable in my hand. I mean, I was serviceable. I could, after a few tries, land a fly in the general vicinity of a rising trout. And I'd caught some decent fish. In fact, the first trout I landed was a drop-dead gorgeous cutthroat. The old man was standing right beside me, him in his waders and me in a pair of jeans, in Little Trappers Lake in Colorado. I must have had the accidental good fortune of drifting a nymph in front of a trout that had given up on life, because he latched on and I all but reeled him through the tiptop of the rod, the old man screaming in my ear the whole time about stripping line and playing the fish to tire him. I'd never understood this idea of playing a fish. I wanted that kamikaze trout in the net, and I wanted him there fast. But I have to say, I don't think I've ever seen the old man happier than the day

I caught my first trout. The wind came up while we hiked the mile and a half back to the campsite, my wet jeans freezing solid around my legs. He wrapped me in a couple of sleeping bags and put me to bed, shivering. I remember smiling and thawing out and thinking that I had this whole fishing thing figured out. I was a young idiot.

That hot afternoon of the talk, the old man gave up on using the bream bed as a metaphor, because his question floated in the air, unanswered. He watched me make a few false casts before I shot my own Woolly Bugger toward the bream beds. It was an ugly cast. Instead of unfurling lazily over the water, the yellow fly line curled on the surface like crazy hieroglyphics. I probably whispered *Damn it!* just loud enough for him to hear.

"You realize you don't have to rush it," my father said. "You're in too much of a hurry. You can't be in a hurry."

He was right. I hadn't hesitated properly in my back cast. My rhythm was all off. I pulled in the slack first, then started hauling the fly through the water. "And stop stripping line so fast. This isn't a race, you know. Everything has its own speed. You're always in such a hurry. Things are going to happen when they happen. When they're supposed to happen. There are things you just can't rush. You understand what I'm saying?"

I've always been a little slow on the uptake. I'd forgotten why we were there. I assumed we were back talking about fishing again. It wasn't until he said, "If you have questions, you can always ask me. I may not be an expert, but I'll tell you what I know, when you need to know it," that I figured out we were discussing something more than how to work a Woolly Bugger through a bream bed.

If I recall, he had a smile on his face at that point, like a man who could finally let go of a breath he'd been holding far too long. He glanced toward the bream bed and clicked some line out of his reel. I watched him cast his fly rod, watched that perfect loop uncoil behind him, then with a smooth snap of his forearm, watched him reverse the loop in the opposite direction, toward the bed. He dropped that Woolly Bugger on the nose of a bream the size of a Frisbee. The fly hadn't sunk three inches before the bream rose and sucked it in and ran away from the bed, no doubt protecting whatever was incubating inside that ring. He played that fish until it gave up, stripping line only when he needed to, as he brought it quietly to the side of the johnboat.

I'm not sure if floating on a lake in the heat of the day and tossing a fly rod toward a bream bed is the ideal way to have the talk with your son. Some child psychologist would probably have a problem with it, probably say I'm scarred for life. But the old man was smart enough to know that fishing was somehow tied in with the larger things of this world, one way or the other. When I saw those gorgeous giant perfect loops spooling off the water when a fly rod was in my father's hands, I knew I'd learned something about what lay ahead of me in the world. The old man taught me everything about fishing. He may have taught me a little bit about everything else I would ever need to know.

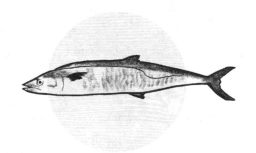

The Year of the Mackerel
MARK POWELL

The year I caught the king mackerel we were living in
Charleston, my wife and I, in a Battery mansion divided
into six elegant, if compact apartments. Living there
had long been a dream of mine. I grew up in the mountains
of Oconee County, South Carolina, the southern sliver of the
Blue Ridge, and had spent the greater part of my days in the
woods walking, and later running, trail after trail.

Charleston had always represented some idealized urban dream,
the moonlight and magnolias, the hansom cabs, the gardens tucked
into pockets of ivy and stone. I'd been to college there, but not quite.

As a cadet at the Citadel, there was always a remove, as much cultural as physical. I was never quite there. So when the opportunity came to return, my wife and I jumped at it. I would be teaching at the College of Charleston. I would be leaving the mountains.

I was fine with that.

Twice in my life I have tried to convince myself that I am a coastal man, a man given to beaches and marsh ponds, to wide skies and blue horizons, a man not hemmed in by mountains. Twice I have almost fooled myself, first in Charleston and years later in Florida, and twice I have come to realize that the deepest part of me belongs in the mountains.

The year I caught the king mackerel was also the year I feared I would fall apart, or perhaps had fallen apart already and had only become aware of it, realizing my own fragility the way you might encounter, say, a broken bone: in a moment of stunned confusion that suddenly articulates itself as pain.

That was the year I was old enough to think things like 'this is your life, right now, what is happening to you,' but not yet old enough to be embarrassed by the naiveté of such. It wasn't a crisis—I understand that now. It was simply a coming to terms with life, a very necessary thing. But at the moment it felt fraught, and my anxiety manifested itself in the "long runs," two and three hours jogging down along the Battery over to East Bay, past the Coast Guard station, past the wharf and the old Slave Market, looping the peninsula as dawn gave way to morning, thinking, praying, considering what was and what wasn't and what might yet be. I ran, and, just as I always had, I ran beside water.

That year, in our antebellum wedding cake of porches and colonnades, I found myself dreaming of water, of immersion, of currents. We were on the third floor, the top floor, and if you pressed your face to the wire grid porch-screen you could see the blue of the harbor through the tops of the winter trees.

Like me, my wife had grown up in the mountains, and we had returned there after school, living in a small cabin on the edge of Sumter National Forest. The water there was the milky green of a mountain lake, a slender dogleg just big enough to ski on in a ragged Glassmaster nearly as old as we were. The water there was the whitewater and still pools of the Chattooga and Chauga Rivers, and just as I would later run along the edge of Charleston harbor, I had spent years running along the banks of both rivers.

I had done my share of fishing, too, trout fishing with my brother James and our friend Karl. Or, more accurately, I had done my share of going fishing, walking down from the Walhalla Fish Hatchery where, as often as not, I would leave my rod and go run along the trails with my dog Buddy. Fishing was an excuse to be in the woods, to be alone in the woods, to linger there because lingering alone in the woods was what I needed. It was never about the fishing.

But that year in Charleston I convinced myself it was.

That year in Charleston I began to pine for the mountains, for the Chattooga, for the slanting wilderness around Lick Log and Yellow Branch Falls. Missing that place, missing that life was not something I welcomed. I had worked to convince myself that what I wanted most was to get out of those mountains, out of that place and out of that life. I wanted the nearest city I could find, and that happened to be Charleston. So that year, when I began to spend less time staring at the water and more time remembering the trees, I told myself it wasn't the place I missed, it was the activity. It was fishing. To go out on the water, to catch a big silvery fish, would be to affirm this new me. So when my wife's parents and sister came down to visit I booked us a half-day fishing trip and that morning, just before dawn, we walked down to the marina where the captain was fueling the boat.

The salt air felt cool, and all around us the darkness was failing. It was a new day and it felt like it. We left at daylight.

We fished along the jetty and out toward the Isle of Palms, but it was only when we were back inside the harbor that something hit my line, exactly as I had imagined it would. When I finally brought it alongside I saw it was exactly what it should be: forty-two inches of flashing light. It floated there, hooked and gaffed, as thin and bright as a blade. When the waves drifted over and past, it flickered like some yet-to-be-realized life, and I knew right then I would have it mounted. That I would hang it in some future Charleston manse. I began to construct the story I would tell, the way it pulled and fought, the impossible bend of my rod as it dived. We put it on ice and made for the marina. I felt triumphant, briefly I felt triumphant.

But by the time it came back from the taxidermist I was back in the mountains.

Nothing had changed for me, and in May we had left Charleston, flying to Europe where my wife and I spent our days burning through what was left of a literature fellowship I'd received the year before. We moved from city to city. I kept running, thinking, praying, but I felt no less settled. That fall we returned to Oconee County where my fish, mounted beautifully, was waiting for me in a box at my father-in-law's store, a general store at the foot of the mountains that specializes in fishing supplies—rods, flies, bait.

I dreaded seeing it. It still felt like a trophy, but a trophy commemorating my failure to escape. I lifted it from the wood shavings and there was no denying its elegance, the clean lines, the impossibly delicate fins. I held it and wondered where we would go next, anxious with possibility. Yet within minutes, I felt something release. I felt myself surrender to myself, to that place, to those mountains. I understood then that though those mountains had made me, though they held me, their hold wasn't suffocating. I realized it never had been. I could come and go, and a part of me would always stay. It wasn't an either/or equation: to live in that tension, in that coming and going, of something but not quite, was to be alive. That this is a dramatic thing to say, that this is a cliché, makes it no less true.

I held my fish and looked around my father-in-law's store.

It's a mountain place, but when I asked him if I could hang my fish there among the mounted trout, the rainbows and browns, he said yes, and it hangs there still, something, I came to realize, that both belongs and doesn't, at least not quite.

And that's what makes it interesting to me. Not that I caught it, but that it hangs in that tension, this sleek saltwater thing there among the fresh. I stop by to see it every time I go up the mountain, and every time I come back down.

Frogging Quintana
NATALIE BASZILE

A few days before I leave for south Louisiana, Patrick calls to say he has a surprise for me. "How'd you like to go frogging?" he asks. "My friend, Jay has agreed to take you if you're interested."

"I'm in," I answer, without thinking twice—because Patrick is my running buddy, my Ace Boon Coon, my concierge for all things south Louisiana. When we're together, we obsess over eighteenth-century antiques, French portraits, sushi, and Acadian architecture. We're equally miserly when it comes to clothes and couldn't give less than a damn about the cars we drive, but if a rare cypress armoire or mahogany tester bed were to come up at auction, we'd both be tempted to sell one of our children. I have a strict policy of saying yes to Patrick's invitations, no matter how crazy they sound, because he loves adventure, has a mischievous streak, and in the Southern storytelling tradition, can spin a yarn like nobody's business. I've heard him tell hilarious stories of near misses and improbable encounters and figure it's about time I see where he gets his material.

Fifty years ago, our friendship wouldn't have been possible. If Louisiana hadn't prohibited a black woman and a white man from being friends, the social pressure would have been unbearable.

"Great," Patrick says. He sounds happy and slightly amused, as if he knows something I don't. "Be sure to pack pants, long sleeves, and some shoes you don't mind getting muddy."

It's after dark, and the sky is filled with glossy stars when Patrick and I pull up in front of a one-story brick house just off Main Street in Franklin. In the driveway, a Toyota Tundra is hitched to a goose-neck trailer on top of which sits an aluminum batteau, a modern version of the flat-bottom wooden boats fur traders used during the colonial days. The garage door is open, so we walk in and climb steps that lead to the kitchen. That's something I've learned about south Louisiana: people rarely enter houses through the front door. Even guests go through the garage or around the side.

"Welcome to the Dog House," Jay says as we step into the kitchen. To my San Franciscan eye, he looks like a farmer—big and boyish, with a doughy face and hands to match.

The place looks strangely unused—no dishes in the sink, no pots on the stove, no appliances on the counter. No plants, no family pictures; none of the extra touches that make a house a home. A bachelor's pad, I'm guessing.

"Why do you call it the Dog House?" I ask.

"This is where I come when my wife gets mad at me and puts me out," Jay says, zipping his camouflage windbreaker. He laughs. "Actually, my father owns this house and uses it mostly for parties and storage." Turns out the Dog House is next door to Cashway, the pharmacy Jay manages. He crashes here when he works late and doesn't feel like driving forty miles to his home in Youngsville.

We load a cooler into the truck bed and set off for the Franklin Canal. The three-quarter moon follows us through the empty streets and across the railroad tracks to the back of town. A truck approaches from the opposite direction.

"Probably just got finished doing what we're about to do," Jay says. Frogging season opened in June. It's mid-July now.

I catch myself wondering what my dad would say if he knew I was riding around the Louisiana countryside with two white guys. My dad hated Louisiana, and for good reason: In the 1950s when he was a teenager and lived in a small town not far from here, he worked at a gas station after school. When he fell asleep on his breaks, the white boys he worked with slathered his bare feet with liquid rubber and set them on fire, then fell over themselves laughing as they watched him hop around trying to extinguish the flames. The night he graduated from high school, he packed his bags and left for California, which is where I was born. But as much as I consider myself a Californian, Louisiana pulls at me. I love it here. I feel rooted. The place is in my blood. There's something waiting in me, something that sits dormant when I'm in San Francisco. If my dad were still alive, that's what I'd tell him.

At the boat landing, it's a Chinese fire drill as Jay slides behind the wheel and climbs into the batteau, and Patrick takes his place as driver. Lots of hand motions and whistling follow as Patrick backs the whole rig down the ramp into the water.

"Not too fast," Jay calls, "or water will come up over the back."

That's another thing I've noticed about south Louisiana: everyone owns a boat, or knows someone who does. In the week I've been here, I've heard folks talk about new trawlers that can navigate the high seas, watched kids jet ski out at the Point, and caught sight of speed boats zipping up and down the bayou behind Patrick's house.

A minute later, the truck is parked and we're all situated in the batteau.

"Who wants a drink?" Jay says. "I've got Michelob Ultra, Bud Light, Coors Light, Abita Light, water, and Gatorade."

Thirty years ago we would have been chugging screwdrivers. *My God*, I think, *we've gotten old.*

Jay cracks open a Bud Light, hands us both waters, then guns the motor. For a few minutes we skim over the canal, light as water bugs. Patrick sits in front, and at this speed, his face becomes a windshield. As we cut through the water, bugs splatter against his forehead, get tangled in his beard.

"I should have brought goggles," he shouts, then swings around to squint out over the bow, the wind blowing his hair, brindled and freshly cut, back from his face.

Jay, meanwhile, is stationed by the Pro Drive, an air-cooled outboard motor that proves perfect for cutting through grasses and water hyacinths. He looks like Cyclops in his lime green helmet with the big spotlight mounted on the front. As he glances from side to side the beam arcs over the water, illuminating the droplets splashing beside us and bathing the trees on either bank in warm yellow light.

"Smell that?" Jay says.

"Willow," Patrick answers before I smell anything. I didn't even know willow *had* a smell. *Who are these guys?* I wonder again, and remind myself that boys here grow up hunting, fishing, and wandering the woods in a way city boys never do. When my dad was a boy, he loved to fish in the pond and hunt in the patch of dense woods behind his house. He carried crawfish he caught, the rabbits and raccoons, possums and squirrels that he shot home to his mother who cooked them in stews. Once he shot and ate a crow.

"I used to spend hours out here when I was a kid," Patrick says, as if he's read my thoughts. "Once, before we had boats with motors, I paddled out here from the bayou near my house. Took me all night."

I close my eyes and inhale the willow's vaguely flowery fragrance, the warm night air like a chamois against my skin.

There's dark and then there's bayou-dark—which is more like the darkness of deep space, I discover, when Jay switches off his headlamp. The banks and even the water vanish and we're floating in black, echoey nothingness. I can't see Patrick though he's right in front of me. I can't see Jay who's somewhere back there. *Please, God, don't let us hit a log and flip this boat*, I think. *I'd have no clue which direction to swim.*

We glide like this for a while. The world out here is infinitely still, but not at all quiet. Crickets and cicadas compete to see who can chirp the loudest, water sloshes against the batteau, and all around us tree frogs croak and groan. Jay steers the boat like a master captain. How he knows where to go is a mystery, but as we cruise along, I feel the space around us open up, and as the moon shifts lower along the horizon, I can tell we're someplace different. The air feels less dense. Sure enough, when Jay flips on his headlamp, we're in a watery intersection as wide as a football field.

Franklin Canal is part of an intricate system of byways originally built to transport logs to the sawmill. Ultimately, the canal leads to the

Intracoastal Waterway. Jay takes a hard left and we swing around in a wide semicircle, out of the intersection and into a narrower canal no wider than a two-lane country road. The air is thick and heavy with mildew and the trees are draped in so much pale gray moss I can barely see the branches.

We come upon someone's fish camp, a small cypress shack built on a dock. That's the third thing I've noticed: these Louisiana men love their camps. They spend hours, sometimes days, in their rustic waterfront man caves, cooking, lounging, telling stories. This one looks ghostly, floating there all creaky and weather-beaten, the two front windows like hooded eyes, the little porch a lazy mouth where it tilts down to meet the water.

Oh my God, I think, *this is exactly like* the Pirates of the Caribbean *ride at Disneyland*. But I keep the thought to myself, not wanting to sound like a tourist. Or a five-year old.

Jay swings the light around, and out of nowhere, a mullet hurls itself from the water into the batteau. It hits the deck with a dull thud, then lies there wide-eyed, silvery, and gasping through pink lips until Patrick tosses it over the side.

The foliage back at the boat ramp was anemic compared to what surrounds us out here. Spanish moss hangs low, like velvety drapes, and the canal is choked with tupelo, cypress, native grasses, and water hyacinths. The water hyacinths were first introduced to Louisiana at the 1888 Cotton Expo in New Orleans, on display at the Japanese Pavilion. Enchanted by the blossoms, people took cuttings home as souvenirs, but then discarded them in the waterways when the novelty wore off. Now the hyacinths choke out native species and clog every waterway in the state. A field of them blocks our passage. Jay glides over as best he can, then cuts through the rest by lifting and lowering the Pro Drive so the blades slice through the leaves. A lot of good *that* does. The moment we pass, the hyacinths close up behind us, our presence erased from history.

"I haven't been out in Quintana in ten years," Patrick says. "We practically lived back here when we were in high school."

"Let's hope we catch something," Jay says. Like any gracious host, he wants to make sure I have a good time, and I can tell from his voice he's getting nervous. But just like that, as if it's been waiting for its cue, a tiny frog no bigger than Jay's thumb lands on his pant leg. "This is exactly what we're looking for," Jay says, sounding hopeful, "only ten times bigger."

Frogging isn't a sport; it's an addiction. As we cruise through Quintana, Jay and Patrick trade stories about how many hours they've spent frogging on a given night—four, five, six—and how many pounds of frog legs they've eaten in one sitting. Patrick tells the story of a friend who started frogging as soon as the sun went down and didn't quit till it came up the next morning. Jay says that out in rice country, where farmers flood the fields, he's caught as many as one hundred twenty frogs in one night. All the time he's been talking, Jay has been turning his head from left to right, his third eye sweeping along one bank and then the other, but now he goes quiet.

"There's one," he says, suddenly serious. "You see it? Right behind that cypress." He trains his lamp on the bank.

"I see it," Patrick says.

I follow the beam of light, but see nothing. No matter—Jay and Patrick are on the case. While Jay steers the boat closer to the bank and trains the beam of light on the spot, Patrick crawls on his belly till he's leaning over the front of the batteau.

I don't see any frogs, but I *do* see a tangle of knobby tree branches, stumps, spikey roots, spider webs, and black mud that looks like it would swallow us whole if we gave it a chance. There's no way our batteau can get in there, but Jay keeps steering us forward, holding the light still, until we're right up on the bank and I hear myself cry, "No way! No way!" as the top half of Patrick's body disappears in the underbrush.

"You got it?"

Patrick doesn't answer for a long time. His body is still. His orange life jacket flows like a flare. Then he inchworms himself back till his knees hit the deck and holds up a fat, grinning bullfrog, as big and juicy as a Porterhouse steak. I scream. I can't help it. The little frog that jumped onto Jay's pant leg was cute in a cartoonish sort of way, but Patrick has dragged a monster into our batteau. Its bulbous black eyes look like chunks of onyx under their partially lowered inner eyelids and stare at me accusingly; its skin, emerald green and dappled with black spots, glistens like enamel; its mouth extends in a lipless line from one side of his head to the other; its legs are fat as a baby's. As long as the spotlight is on it, though, the frog is hypnotized and won't move. That's the secret, the guys tell me, and I want desperately to believe them.

I need time to digest what I've gotten myself into. I could be back at Patrick's, sipping a Pimm's Cup and flipping through an auction catalogue as the bayou drifts by, but *nooooo*, I had to be bold, try something new. I remember what my dad used to say: you go looking for adventure, sometimes all you find is disaster.

Jay opens the purple crawfish sack that will serve as our case, and after Patrick drops the frog in, he knots the opening and loops it through the cooler's handle just as the frog realizes what's happened to him and leaps angrily, bumping against the side of the cooler, the side of the batteau, until he's exhausted. One frog down, who knows how many to go. Patrick uses a long pole with what looks like a duck's bill on the end to push us away from the bank. As soon as we're dislodged and floating free, Jay guns the motor and we're off. The hunt has begun.

• • •

The night deepens. The moon has turned the color of orange sherbet, and the air feels like a warm bath. Jay strips off his camouflage windbreaker, down to his t-shirt, while Patrick rolls up his sleeves. Farther down Quintana, a sweetgum tree has fallen across the canal. For a moment, it looks like we won't go any further, but then Jay sees that someone has cut one of the branches. With some expert maneuvering, we're on the other side, only to discover a banana spider has spun her web across the width of the canal. She hangs there, big and black, right in the center of her masterpiece, and we have to duck to miss it.

Patrick shivers. "That's the worst feeling, walking into a spider's web."

And with that, the storytelling portion of the evening begins. For the next twenty minutes, Jay and Patrick trade tales of their most frightening nature encounters, their accents thickening the longer they speak.

Jay's headlamp sweeps over a raccoon scrounging for dinner on the far bank. An alligator, his nose the length of a shotgun barrel, drifts towards us, curious to see what all the fuss is about. Patrick and Jay tempt it by leaning over the side and splashing their hands in the water, but I don't think it's funny. The other day at Patrick's, his boys teased an alligator by casting their bobber into the water and reeling it in fast as they could, the alligator in hot pursuit. I've never seen an animal move so fast.

"I've seen gators swim fast enough to keep up with a boat," Jay says, then recounts the recent news story about a swamp guide whose hand was bitten off when he tried to demonstrate, by dangling a piece of chicken, how high an alligator could jump out of the water. We all laugh nervously, imagining the boatload of horrified tourists, but I grab Patrick's collar and pull him back just in case.

"There's another one," Jay says, shining his light, and it's back to work.

This time, the frog is floating on a sea of duckweed—green, clover-shaped algae that blankets the water's surface. Jay trains his spotlight and suddenly I see what he sees: another fat frog, his eyes glowing silvery-white as aluminum foil in the light, his underbelly the color of a marshmallow. Patrick assumes his position, Jay drives us forward, and Bingo! Another frog drops into the sack.

It's illegal to catch frogs with anything but your hands, a net, or something called a "gig," a small pitchfork attached to a long pole. So when we spot a frog way back in a forest of cypress knees, Patrick grabs the gig and stands on the bow like Neptune as Jay pushes the batteau as far forward as it will go. I can just see the frog. He's crouched and frozen, dazzled by the glare, soothed by the spotlight's sudden warmth. Patrick leans forward, raises the gig like a spear, and takes aim. *What a way to go*, I think.

Jay is apologetic. "It's gory, but we try to be humane," he says. "We only use the gig when we have to."

I guess he thinks that since I'm from peace-loving San Francisco, I'll object. But I'm not squeamish, and besides, all this excitement has my blood running. "Don't worry," I say. "I've seen worse," and tell him about the bullfight my husband and I went to in Spain on our honeymoon. Maybe an appreciation for life's cycles is what I inherited from my dad. Maybe this is one reason Louisiana has always felt like home.

Six or seven more frogs, then the guys tell me it's my turn. Jay finds the perfect specimen—not too big and not too small—lounging in an open space on the bank. It's mesmerized by the spotlight, and as Jay steers closer, I trade places with Patrick and assume the position. Closer, then closer still, till I'm a few inches away and that frog and I are looking each other in the eye.

"Grab it," Patrick yells.

"Grab it," Jay echoes, "Quick!"

Until this moment, I've been one of the boys, hurtling through the night, tooling up and down the murky canal, not caring how my hair looks or whether I have big sweat rings under my arms, laughing at tales of swamp guides stupid enough to taunt alligators with chicken breasts. In some ways, I've gone further in two hours than my dad was able to do in a lifetime. But suddenly, I'm queasy. I can't make my arms move. All I can think about is the feel of that slimy, clammy frog skin in my hand. My head throbs with imaginary croaking.

"Grab it!" Patrick yells again.

It feels like forever that I'm hanging over the front of this batteau. Jay's spotlight illuminated a wide circle of ground around me, and for a second I think the sun has come up. I feel its warmth on my back, on my neck, on my arms, which are supposed to be reaching, but are instead plastered against my sides, rigid as bayonettes.

"Grab it!" The batteau rocks gently as Patrick stands up to see what's happening, why I'm not moving. And then something shifts. The trance is broken. The frog leaps away.

"Ah man, she girled out on us," Patrick says.

It's true.

I inch backward and take my seat on the bench, my tail between my legs. "I couldn't do it," I say. "I couldn't make my arms move."

"That's O.K." Patrick squeezes my shoulder. "At least you tried."

If I were a dude, they'd never let me hear the end of it, but since I'm not, they go easy on me. As if he were my big brother, Jay offers to let me wear the headlamp again while he and Patrick catch half a dozen more frogs, and by the time we turn toward home an hour later, fifteen bullfrogs are stepping over each other trying to climb out of the sack.

Three hours of frogging. It's almost midnight. We cut back up Quintana and out into the bigger canal, Jay's headlamp sweeping over the far banks where alligator eyes flash like brake lights. We re-hitch the boat and head home. Back at the Dog House, I shake Jay's hand and hug him.

"I'll never forget this," I say. "Thank you so much."

"Anytime," he says, yawning. It's Tuesday night. He has to get up for work in the morning. Luckily, he only has to walk next door.

Patrick is still amped up when he drops me off at my cottage. "So what did you really think?"

"I loved it," I say, and I don't just mean the frogging—I mean all of it.

My dad had a change of heart in the last year of his life. He wanted to make one last trip, to say goodbye to the parts of Louisiana he loved and wanted to remember—the land, the sky, the water, the food. He died before he could make the trip. But I'm here now, and I realize Louisiana is different; equally complicated, but easier, in some ways, to love.

Truth or Consequences:
The One That Didn't Get Away
MICHAEL FARRIS SMITH

When I was a kid, my summer vacations consisted of loading up the family Buick, and then driving from South Mississippi to Griffin, Georgia, which is my father's hometown. Me and my two sisters crowded into the backseat and then tried not to irritate the hell out of each other, and my parents, during the seven-hour drive. We always went in August, driving to my grandmother's small house, where we would then spend the next week visiting aunts and uncles and cousins.

Another big part of our trip was taking day trips to Atlanta. We loved the Braves, no matter how horrendous they were in those days, and we also visited Stone Mountain and Six Flags each year. Despite the predictability of our late summer vacation, my sisters and I loved it. We always went to Atlanta Fulton County Stadium early to watch batting practice, we stayed until dark at Stone Mountain for the laser light show, and we ate pounds of sweet Georgia barbecue.

But the summer when I was ten years old, I found out something I liked a little more than the day trips to amusement parks. Way out in Spalding County, my kin folk had a farm, and though I had been out there many times, I had never known about the small lake located at the end of the dirt road that split the rolling pastures. Everyone was there for a big family cookout later in the evening, and during the afternoon I followed my cousins as they walked out toward the lake carrying a tackle box, rods, and reels.

My cousins were teenagers and I thought they were cool, so when one of them offered me one of the rods, I proudly accepted. It was one of those typical August days in the Deep South, hot and humid with nearly no breeze. The bank was dusty and dry as we spread out around the lake and only the random cloud passing in front of the sun gave us any relief from the blistering day. The lake was well-stocked and it didn't take long for some luck. We brought in bream and a few small bass and I began to feel like a big shot, hanging out with my older cousins, listening to them chat about girls and football and getting drivers licenses. Shirts off, under the sun, catching fish. Suddenly roller coasters and laser shows didn't sound like so much fun.

The afternoon wore on, the sun falling low in the sky, and our young stomachs were ready for the grilled hamburgers and hot dogs planned for the evening. We were right about to pack up when my cousin on the far side of the lake began to wrestle with something big. The rod bowed and there were big splashes and he was hollering out. Look at this, look at this. He moved along the bank, struggling to bring in the big one, right about the time the line snapped. The rod jerked straight up and when the tension broke, his weight carried him backward a couple of clumsy steps before he landed on his rear end. The water went calm, and we all stared at the ripples, imagining what swam beneath.

"Did y'all see that?" he called out. And, of course, we had seen it. There was a whopper out there somewhere.

Walking back toward the house, my cousins decided they had to come back the next day, and the day after, and so on, as long as it took to catch the one that got away. I listened and nodded, knowing tomorrow I was supposed to go with my family to Atlanta. The Braves were playing the Phillies, and my dad would want to go early and eat chili dogs at The Varsity downtown before going to the stadium. I wanted to go, but I didn't want to go. I wanted to hang out with the teenagers and catch that thing. So that's what I did.

All the next morning, my mother kept asking me if I was sure I wanted to stay and fish. And I was because I had barely slept the night before, today's adventure alive in my head. I saw myself being the hero, raising the mighty fish over my head while my cousins slapped me on the back and envied my newfound skills. There was absolutely no way, despite my love for the hapless Atlanta Braves, that I was going to miss the day at the lake.

By mid-afternoon, we not only had not caught the big one, but it was as if the rest of the fish had gotten together and determined that our success the day before was as good as it was going to get. Only random bites here and there, nothing large enough to keep. And my cousins weren't talking about girls and cars anymore, either, but instead were mute with the frustration of our lack of accomplishment. The day seemed hotter and the air felt thicker when the fish weren't participating. I stood on the bank and cast again and again and couldn't help but wonder if my dad was letting my sisters get fried peach pies after their chili dogs, and if this would've been the night a Major League foul ball finally fell into my hands.

I moved along the bank, hoping to find the right spot, and settled in the shade of a small tree. I kept casting, kept losing, getting a little madder each time, believing I had made the wrong decision. And in my anger I decided to really let one fly, to see if I could land the hook way out there, where the big one could only be, and in my recklessness I reared back and brought the rod right through the tree branches. I tugged, but my line was caught up and was not letting go, and a wave of embarrassment swept over me. I'd have to call one of them over to help. I'd have to look like I didn't know what I was doing. I'd have to be a little kid. And I didn't want any of that.

I looked around and none of the others had noticed, so I yanked a few more times and then the line snapped, and it hung there in the tree like a strange and twisted spider web. Again I looked, and again none of them had noticed. But I would have to cross the lake to my cousin with the tackle box, explain what happened, and then sit there while he gave me a new hook and worm. If I ever wanted to come fishing with them again, I didn't think that was a good idea. So instead I did what many good fishers have done before, and what many good fishers will do again.

I lied.

Underneath the tree, I spotted a large rock, the size of a grapefruit. I picked it up and moved away from the tree, back to an empty spot of the bank where I'd stood among the weeds before. I then checked to make sure none of my cousins were watching, and I threw the rock out into the lake as far as I could, making a big splash, and then just as the rock went gulp down into the water, I yanked back on my rod as if I had just lost a mighty battle. Their eyes rose and I yelled out.

"I had him! I swear I had him!"

"What happened?" one of my cousins called back.

"I had him and then he broke my line, too. Just like yesterday. It had to be the same one."

"The big one?"

"Yeah. The big one. I had him."

I don't know whether they believed me or not. A few more questions came across the lake and I answered them like any good liar, with some detail and with a little emotion, trying not to be overdramatic but trying to make it count, and then I tromped around to the other side to get another hook. But by the time I got there, we had all decided we'd had enough. The big one wasn't going to be caught today, or any of its friends. And we headed back to the house, sweaty and silent, in a broken trail of defeat.

But somehow, I felt like I had won. Because I had learned the most important rule of fishing. Whether you catch it or lose it, lie about it.

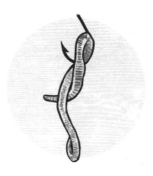

Bait

CHRIS OFFUTT

I grew up on dirt roads surrounded by the Daniel Boone National Forest in the hills of eastern Kentucky. The land is imprinted deep within me. Half of what I know came from being in the woods alone. I've always embraced that part of myself, the background of a rural life. For many years I referred to myself as a "country boy," but at age sixty, that designation might be a little far-fetched. It's hard to call yourself a boy with gray hair, bifocals, a pot belly, and going deaf to boot. But "country man" doesn't have the same connotation. What I am is a guy who lives on fourteen acres and stays away from town. I love my wife and rely on her tremendously, but I do treasure the times she leaves the house. I don't even know where she goes.

Most people grow up in small towns, suburbs, and cities. Their concept of rural life is informed by depictions on TV and movies (terrible portrayals), books they have read (fewer set in the country are published each year), and vacation trips to exotic rural destinations. Americans have become tourists of nature. You can always spot the visitors to a beach town, a ranch, the Delta, or the mountains—they're the ones dressed in clothes that look like movie ideas of what country people wear. Broad plaid shirts, expensive boots, even the occasional set of suspenders. Nothing is broken in. Some clothes still retain the horizontal marks where they were folded at the store. Belts are the final confirmation—way too narrow, with no telltale scrape from a knife clip.

Sporting equipment is the true gold mine of country tourism: guns and ammo, rods and reels. Electronic "fish finders" are available for a price that ranges from a couple of hundred dollars to three thousand. The idea is that instead of enjoying the sky and water—an intrepid fishermen stares at a small screen and waits for a sound that indicates a fish is near.

Tackle boxes are another remarkable market, as if following the twin American maxims: bigger is better, and expensive is impressive. Top of the line is a "bait and tackle prep station" available for $6,000, plus tax and shipping. I have to say, it's pretty nice, and I wanted one immediately after seeing photographs in a brochure. I'm a sucker. At the same time, my own tackle box is eighteen years old, fully functional, and cost fifty cents at a yard sale.

When city people learn about my background, they make a variety of assumptions. My general appearance encourages them because my hair often resembles what's known as a mullet. In my youth, such a style had no name. It was a pragmatic haircut for the woods—short in the front so it wouldn't catch limbs and briars, long in the back to keep rain out of my shirt collar. I drive a truck, live on a dirt road, and wear boots year round. I'm also formally against washing blue jeans. One assumption town-folk make about me is that I possess arcane skills with a chainsaw, axe, and tourniquets, and might be able to hypnotize snakes. The primary assumption is that I am what's known as a "sportsman," meaning a hunter and a fisherman.

In the spirit of disclosure, I have not walked in the woods with a firearm since I left the hills of Kentucky. My technique for fishing is to bait a hook, cast the line, and watch the bobber until I get bored—usually about forty seconds. There's always something better to look at. Sunlight on the water, drifting clouds, or birds in the sky watching me watch them. Frankly, the word "bobber" is misleading in its optimism. Most of the time it doesn't do any bobbing at all. It just floats, and will eventually drift into a snag. Usually I prop my rod on a forked stick, then wander the bank looking for attractive rocks.

As a child in the hills I gathered nightcrawlers in the evening after a light rain, carrying a flashlight and a bucket. In Mississippi my technique for harvesting nightcrawlers proved ineffective. Maybe I needed an electronic worm finder! I thought I'd lost some essential woodscraft, or maybe the worms here were smart enough to avoid humans. I resolved to purchase worms, an act of rural betrayal. It's like work gloves—if you need to wear them, you probably shouldn't be doing the work.

The closest store to my house sells gasoline, propane, ice, barbeque, beer, milk, Pringles, Vienna sausages, and an array of Little Debbie snacks. Once a week they have corn dogs. A low shelf holds two child-size life jackets, bright orange and covered with dust. They've been there for at least three years because kids here learn early to fend for themselves. Mississippi parents coddle their kids by waiting until their eighth birthday for a first gun. (In Kentucky, we arm children at age six.)

The store's biggest section is dedicated to fishing gear. For two dollars, you can buy a quart of dirt in a Styrofoam container and twelve nightcrawlers. The worms are long enough that you can wrap your entire hook and still leave an end trailing in the water, or you can tear each worm in half and double your fishing time. As a cheapskate, I usually go for the latter. (The record for earthworm length is twenty-two feet, found in South Africa in 1967. They're still fishing with it.) Recently I asked the store clerk about the provenance of the nightcrawlers.

As it turned out, the worms were from Canada. This fact astounded me and I nearly dropped my Honey Bun. The closest Canadian town is Windsor, Ontario, which is a thousand miles away, and I wondered what the profit margin was at sixteen cents per worm. Expenses included labor, containers, trucking, border fees, and gasoline. How was it possible to make money with all that transportation? Did fluctuating fuel costs affect the price of nightcrawlers? Did worms trickle down with a change in the economy? If the USA ended NAFTA, would worm prices soar?

Fortunately, my personal library is extensive enough to include a 40-year-old privately printed pamphlet about raising earthworms. My perusal provided me with more information than I thought was possible. In the interest of space and boredom, here's the crucial fact—worms are extremely cheap to raise. The start-up cost is minimal, consisting of a bin with a lid, dirt, and two worms. Eventually you will have castings, which you can sell as well. I wasn't familiar with the term "castings" but found a long-winded definition that referred to the residue excreted from the alimentary canal. Apparently worm manure is the richest fertilizer on the planet. Worm farmers sell castings at a premium, which would certainly offset the cost of shipping live worms to Mississippi.

The more I read, the more I considered getting into commercial earthworms. Buckets of dirt lead to buckets of cash—selling worms, selling the dirt itself, and selling the doo-doo. All you need is two worms to start. Luckily, earthworms are bi-sexual hermaphrodites so you don't have to worry about pairing the genders. (Or which bathroom they're supposed to use.) Just get hold of two worms and they'll figure out the rest, like teenagers.

My wife is from Texas and is pretty tough. She also has staunch ideas regarding what transpires in the house, and what happens outside. We are often at odds over this, and I always lose. For example, she keeps her dogs indoors, which is a violation of my country principles. She also likes to turn the air conditioning to a chilly temperature, then lie on the couch beneath a blanket—with dogs. None of it makes sense to me. Worst of all, she sees the garage as a place to park her car, not raise earthworms. As a result of her peculiarities, my commercial enterprise ended before it began.

I still fish though, and I bite the bullet and buy the damn worms. My property includes a big pond that had been stocked by a previous owner. I've caught bream, catfish, and carp. A couple of times it was clear to me that a very large fish lurked the depths, evidenced by the force with which it struck. I reeled in nothing—the worm, hook, and part of the line had vanished. I resolved to stalk that creature, and reasoned that it prowled the deepest part, in the center of the pond. At the store I bought heavy-duty line and rewound it on my reel. I got a hook like a small anchor, so heavy it required a buoy instead of a bobber.

One evening, near dusk, I slowly rowed to the middle of the pond and baited the hook with fifteen worms. I wrapped them and tied them and skewered them until the hook was totally obscured. Very gently I eased my squirming lump of bait overboard. The sunset was gorgeous but I maintained tight focus on the task at hand. I ignored the call of whippoorwill, the racket of frogs, and the rattling of cicadas. Nothing mattered but catching Mister Big Fish.

It struck with a ferocity that jerked the rod hard enough to pop one of my shoulders from its socket. I shrugged it back in place and gripped the pole. The boat began moving, dragged by the fish in a zig-zag fashion that increased in velocity. I braced my boots and leaned backward. The fish pulled the boat toward the low branch of a maple hanging over the water..I ducked but the limb gouged my scalp and tore out a chunk of hair. Blood streamed into my eyes but I didn't care. That son of a bitch was mine. It didn't occur to me that the fish was thinking the same way.

My arms quivered from exertion. My hands ached from grasping the pole, which bent back and forth in the air, almost to the breaking point before moving the other direction. Eventually the fish wearied, or so I thought. But really, it was just tired of its own game. It began swimming extremely fast for the far bank, towing the boat at a rate that produced a chop. At the last second, the fish swerved hard, pulling an underwater U-turn, whipping the boat around. I dropped the rod, which got hung on the oarlock. The boat struck the bank with enough force to throw me out. I landed hard on the back of my head.

When I regained consciousness, it was full dark. I staggered into the house, more exhausted than I'd ever felt in my life. My head had sustained two wounds—fore and aft—and my back was bruised. My wife was gone, God knows where, and I was grateful that she couldn't witness my humiliation. I took a shower, dressed my wounds, and crawled into bed. I slept eleven hours. By nature I'm a lousy sleeper, so this was a champion effort.

In the morning I limped to the pond. My boat was gone. Skid marks in the mud led back to the water. I understood that the fish had dragged it into the pond and sunk it. Later, I told my wife I'd sold the boat. To prove it, I took her out to lunch. Then she suggested we go shopping. Since she believed I was flush from the boat sale, I had to agree. That fish kept costing me money—a boat, rod and reel, then a fancy dress—and forced me to lie to my wife. I never fished that pond again. I never told this story before, either. Sometimes when I can't sleep I imagine the fish telling the story to his wife. He doesn't have to take her out to lunch to prove it.

Shark Bait

LEIGH ANN HENION

"I t's night, so there will be sharks out hunting," the onboard biologist says as he hands me a flashlight. Already, I have been issued a full-body wetsuit, because Australia is on the verge of killer jellyfish season. As if this isn't inauspicious enough: I've traveled to the other side of the planet in order to witness something that might not happen for weeks.

The synchronized spawning of coral on the Great Barrier Reef is believed to be connected to the cycles of the moon. When it happens each spring, near the equinox, coral release trillions of eggs and sperm sacs simultaneously. These reproductive materials form slicks that appear as cherry blossom flotsam, sometimes in concentrations so dense they're visible from space.

The spawning, one of the most spectacular sights on earth, wasn't discovered until 1981.

And it's nearly as mysterious now as it was back then.

In corner stores and on boat docks across the state of Queensland, people have been making predictions, taking bets on when the coral's going to party. I've come at the right time of year, but predicting the spawning isn't an exact science. "Sometimes," the biologist says, "the spawning takes place in areas and nobody even knows."

Flynn Reef—one of the 2,900 that make up the Great Barrier—is soon just a few feet from my chest. In the diffused beam of my flashlight, I can make out fish hiding in coral crevices. I am especially thrilled to see a green turtle—until I notice the shark-bite-shaped chunk missing from its back.

Not ten minutes after I jump in, my flashlight—my only distress call— goes on the fritz. It fizzles until it leaves me in complete darkness. I hit it against my neoprene-covered palm until it stutters back to life.

But not before I've lost my bearings.

In the distance, I can see a second boat, one of the few other opera- tors who have decided to make a run in case this is the big night. The moon is contributing to my confusion. It's red and swollen. I've been told its appearance is due to bushfires.

From here, it looks like the entire universe is ablaze.

In lieu of catching sea life in a net, I've suspended myself in the ocean's web. There isn't an inch of my body that isn't communing with creatures. Gelatinous beings wiggle in front of my face. They are mag- nificently strange, spreading internal light as they slip through the water.

I'm weightless, floating in space.

Every so often, scuba divers move through the sometimes-passable swath between me and the reef. Bubbles released from their tanks mix in with the mercurial, translucent life all around me and tickle my face.

Two older members of the group are attached to a life preserver that's being towed by an instructor. The prop makes them discernible among nameless heads, bobbing like dark apples in the ocean. Abruptly, one of them screams, "*Shark!*"

It takes me a second to realize she's not kidding.

I throw my fins on the deck of the closest boat and pull myself out to take a seat next to a local woman who failed to borrow a stinger suit. A non-lethal welt is forming on her arm. She says it's a small price to pay to commune with coral.

Last year, the spawning happened while she was in the water. The event was so massive there was a meter of eggs on the surface when she emerged from free diving. She tells me that, from underwater, the eggs looked like pink, sky-bound snow. She says, "I love the spawning because there's a mystery to it. They don't know how the coral know to spawn together. Also, people don't think of coral as an animal, and the spawning is a reminder that it's alive."

Coral, classified as a plant until the eighteenth century, are brainless animals that have a full seventy percent of DNA in common with humans. During the spawning, hundreds of diverse species release reproductive materials at the same time. But, without brains, how do they know how? There have been recent revelations that coral have photoreceptors, precursors to eyes. This has helped scientists in their quest to figure out how the spawning is triggered by the moon, temperatures, and tides.

The coral don't *know* when to spawn. They sense it.

The Great Barrier Reef is an ecosystem that's been millennia in the making. It is composed of tiny polyps that have—generation after generation—worked together to build a living skeleton that shelters 1,500 species of fish and 4,000 types of mollusks. The spawning is an annual celebration of interconnected life, eggs and sperm thrown into the water like rice and streamers at a wedding. Each event is a promise fulfilled, one generation building on what was created by the last.

The phenomenon is at its most dazzling here, but there are spawnings in places as unexpected as Egypt and as accessible as Florida. It's predicted that, in the next ten years, ninety percent of these animal colonies will be at risk. I find it hard to accept that both the discovery of this reef's genesis and the destruction of its very life will occur in the span of one generation—mine.

Below deck, someone shouts: "It's happening!"

There are small particulates swirling behind the boat. "Those look like eggs right where we're supposed to jump in!" the voice says. "Definitely eggs!" When it's my turn to enter the water, I can't make out any pink foam.

Instead, I see dozens of iridescent jellyfish.

The woman in front of me shines her flashlight onto the surface. The jellyfish are pulsating, seemingly electric. "They're gorgeous!" she exclaims. When the stranger turns to look at me, I realize that I'm clutching my flippers to my chest. She's going in. I'm next.

"Don't think of the danger," she says. "Focus on the beauty."

I slip into infested waters, only to realize that a nerve-induced pause has cost me my assigned safety group yet again. When I spot the epaulette shark, I'm alone, free floating.

It curves its way around a clump of coral with copper-toned grace. Soon, the shark is directly below me. My flashlight is drawing fish like a lure. We're peacefully suspended there, prey and predators, night swimming together—until the epaulette attacks.

I came to witness the coral spawning.

I ended up helping a shark catch her dinner.

In the distance, I hear a guide convincing one of his bedraggled members to stay out a little longer. I follow his voice. "If you can wait just a second, there's something I'd like to show you," he says. "Cover your light and shake your hand in the water."

The stifled beam makes our hands glow pink as coral eggs. When we wave at each other underwater, the movement sets off faint, bioluminescent stars. Below, a white-tipped shark nearly brushes my thigh. But I don't think of the danger. I'm too focused on the beauty that's slipping through our fingers.

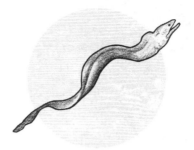

Fishing Lessons:
An Essay in Two Acts
GABINO IGLESIAS

Act I

I'm standing thirty feet from the water in Isla Verde, Puerto Rico. The Atlantic laps at the shore and I feel it in my core. I'm standing roughly nine miles from San Juan and La Perla, the Caribbean version of Ciudad Juárez, three miles from the Luis Lloréns Torres projects, the largest and deadliest in the Caribbean, and about a mile from where I grew up and went to school. This is home. I have jeans on because, despite being at the beach, I'm not here to take a dip. There's a shoebox at my feet. The logo on it would be recognized by almost everyone. Instead of tennis shoes, there's stolen jewelry in the box. Thick gold chains, too-big rings, and a few massive bracelets. I'm sure the majority of it is fake, but young idiots like me go for it anyway.

I should be elsewhere. I have no business selling hot jewelry at the beach in the middle of a weekday. Still, here I am. Things I ignore: where the jewelry comes from, whose pockets the money ends up in, how young thug wannabes/reggaetón singers who've never recorded a single song find me. Things I know: this makes me feel like a badass. I don't have the guts to ask for more, to tell the man who hooked me up with this gig that I'm ready to take a gun from him and go scare someone. However, I have enough guts to do this, to scrape the first layer of the street life with tremulous fingernails while pretending to be a tough guy.

This is probably my fourth or fifth day doing this. It's an easy gig. People show up, we find a hidden corner where the gigantic buildings push against the sand, and rich folks have built tall walls to keep us poor folks out of their pools, show folks what I have (everything has a small white tag hanging from it the way they would at a store), collect the dough, and turn it in at the end of the day to the man who gave me the box. Easy. This day, things get complicated.

The kid is older than me, but not by much. He's slightly taller than me and thinner. His acne has surely made him the butt of many jokes. He's wearing a hoodie at the beach. He looks stupid. No one wears a hoodie to the beach in the Caribbean except terminal junkies and idiots trying to look hard. He stops in front of me and snorts snot into the back of his skull. Then he lifts his chin and pulls the hoodie up a few inches. I see the black, blocky hindquarters of a gun. Something cold squeezes the back of my neck so hard I feel my lips are going to reach my earlobes.

Learning that masculinity is a feeble construct is something you do by reading a lot of smart literature in college or by having someone bash your own masculinity to smithereens in a second. I mumble something, some words I can't recall right now, at least not with the clarity with which I recall the guy's acne scars. In any case, my words sound like an apology, like a weak imploration. They make me angry. I shouldn't be asking this guy for mercy. I should be popping him in the face, taking the gun from him, and beating his teeth down his throat with it. None of that is happening. Instead, the cold thing behind me is still squeezing and I'm so nervous the words coming out of my mouth are pouring out on their own, without control, without filter, without dignity. The guy tells me to take a few steps back. I follow orders like a soldier, my strong dislike for authority melting into the space between wanting to stay alive and the cold thing squeezing the back of my head. The guy picks up the box and mumbles a threat I barely understand. I nod like it's the best idea I've ever heard.

The guy who got me the gig understands. He knows how things go down in the streets. He offers me a job working with his dad at the docks in Old San Juan. His dad takes stuff off shipping boats and "finds" things every week. I've worn shirts pulled from boxes that fell into his car and, years later, would stash a couple of home theatres in my mom's house that had somehow found their way into his hands, but I politely decline the offer.

Days go by and what went down at the beach sticks with me. I'm angry. I should've kicked that guy's ass. I punked out. Then something strange happens: my brain starts telling me I did the right thing.

If overthinking were a disease, I would've died by the time I was fifteen. The mugging lives on in my head and a plethora of scenarios play out, but the idea that I did the right thing keeps growing, keeps whispering itself to me. I let it do its thing. Thinking I was smart somehow feels better than thinking I was a coward. A coward who hadn't yet touched a gun and had a few broken teeth from fights that hadn't always gone as smooth as they had gone in his head before the first punch was thrown.

Time does its thing and keeps on keeping on.

A few weeks later, I go to the same beach with some friends. The beach is close to school and I can walk there from my house, so we do this often. This time, the mood is different. Tanned skin all around, Bob Marley on the tiny radio like some jewel we constantly borrow from the Jamaicans, and girls in bikinis feeding ideas into my adolescent brain. Looking back at the mugging is easy in that context. I survived. Looking at the water, I realize fear hadn't been the only element pushing me to make the right decision.

I was about ten, fishing with my father off an abandoned pier near Luquillo. It was a gray day and the ocean looked irritated. We hadn't caught anything and were starting to pack our stuff when I got a hit. I pulled out a ten-inch moray eel, black and yellow and very angry. It looked cool, all shiny and svelte. I asked my dad to help me with it and throw it in the bucket. He asked me why the bucket if we weren't going to eat it. I said I wanted to keep it. He didn't say a word about us not having anything remotely resembling a place where I could keep it.

A few hours later, the moray eel was on the bottom of a small plastic tank, on its side, opening its mouth weirdly. My dad said it would die soon if I didn't return it to the water. I didn't want to do that. I wanted to keep it, to own it, to show it to my friends. I also didn't want its death over my head. Thinking about the ghost of a moray eel hovering above me freaked me out. I was young, but not so young that I couldn't understand how the things that you kill haunt you forever. I knew the thing had to go back before it was too late. It had started raining in that hard, sideways kind of way that I've only seen in the Caribbean, but my dad drove me back to the pier anyway.

Years later, sitting at the beach still processing something that scared me to the core, I realize that the quiet lesson I learned that day with the moray eel stayed with me: *right decisions don't always feel right*, but staying alive and keeping other things alive feels better than anything.

Act II

The sky above us is as big as the silence between us. It's a sacred silence, the kind that can only exist comfortably between friends who have reached an understanding that goes beyond words. As with all perfect things, the silence doesn't last long.

Luis and I have been inseparable for many years. I will eventually write him and Javi into a novel, but that's something I don't know yet. At the moment, our lines are in the water as we gently paddle up and down Guanica's inlet. His voice comes from a place deep inside him, a place where he exists beyond our current state: two lost kids out of high school trying hard to ignore the monster in front of us.

The words come fast and clear. There's a girl. We all know her. She likes to party. Her veins are always thirsty for warm dreams. Now she's pregnant. The baby is Luis'. He's freaking out.

I fill the silence after his declaration with dumb stuff I've heard in movies and read in books. None of it matters. I think I'm going to college. I want to be the first person in my family to get a degree. Luis is about to have a kid and needs to find a job. She says she's quitting the junk, but he's not sure she can pull it off.

At one point, after the silence comes back, I think he weeps a bit. Then I get a bite and chaos makes everything else disappear because a nine-pound yellow jack can make you feel like he can swim forever while pulling two losers in a red canoe behind. I ended up catching two yellow jacks that day. Beautiful fish. Good eating. It would also be the last time we fished together.

Imagine you can jump through time and land in a tiny, cold room in

Austin, Texas, about a dozen years down the road. I have an ear infection. Something akin to the sound of dirty water dripping from a pipe in a dark basement is going on inside my left ear. The heater is busted and it's a cold winter by Texas standards. My 285-square-feet studio is a not-too-cozy thirty-eight degrees, according to the gray thermometer on my built-in bookshelf. I'm reading an Everett Ruess book when the pain allows and thinking about that day on the water when the pain is too much or the dripping gets too loud.

You see, days on the water stick with you. Some because of what you caught, some thanks to the company, some because of what they meant. That last day on the water with Luis, two kids grew up and a friendship drowned. We didn't kill it and didn't want it dead, but the homies who ride or die with you are rarely the same after a decade of hard living wedges itself between you. Eventually, if you pay attention, those gone days can still be found inside you, and they sometimes hide a lesson inside them, something like a pearl you never knew was there.

Slow the fuck down. How's that for a pearl? I wasn't the one who cried because I was having a kid immediately after high school. I went to college. I got to move on, to visit other countries and meet new friends. I have the patience and reverence for serene moments I developed while fishing to thank for that.

The water is a miraculous thing. You give it your time and patience and it sometimes gives you fish in return. Or not. Maybe it fills you up with zen. Maybe it surreptitiously steals a piece of your heart along with your time. Maybe it invades your soul and stays there forever, sometimes rocking you to sleep and sometimes dripping inside your ear just to remind you that it's there, that it knows where you've been, and that whatever comes next is as mysterious as what you'll pull from its dark belly. And that's okay.

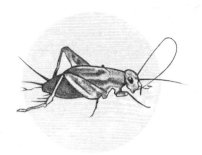

Past the Banks
RAY MCMANUS

L ike a lot of kids in the South, I learned how to fish from my dad. I carried my Zebco and small tackle box of assorted hooks and rubber worms and stinky pieces of god-knows-what and walked behind him on the banks of just about every pond in Lexington County, South Carolina (I had no idea how big the county was back then). We fished bream mostly, sometimes bass, sometimes catfish. Typical stuff really. Typical as a father and son casting out in opposite directions, neither really saying a word to each other.

Like a lot of kids in the South, I learned how to fish from my dad, but everything I learned *about* fishing, I learned from a friend. Up to the point I met Glen, I had fished some big rivers and the occasional mountain stream. I fished the ocean once, some saltwater bays, but always with older men, either from my parents' church or a friend's relative, present. Like my dad, they didn't talk much either. All a kid had to do was watch and repeat. Soon enough, that kid would be hoping to get a bite just because pulling anything in the boat or on the shore meant there would be some excitement, an "atta boy" coupled with some hyperbolic expression about the size of the catch.

Like a lot of kids in the South, I was hungry for an accolade, I'll admit it. But with Glen, fishing wasn't about stroking ego. We were close to the same age. We worked together at the local grocery store. I was in college getting a degree in English and working in the produce department; he was cutting meat and throwing knives at the wall. I was already in a doomed marriage and he was just beginning. Glen went to military school, and I probably should have. He grew up near rivers and marsh. I had ponds and the lake.

Funny how we grow into the bodies of water we are born near. Rivers are constantly moving, changing, but moving in one direction. Lakes, though more still than rivers, rise and fall, hold secrets in their depths—what you see is not always what you get. That was us—Glen, constantly moving, and me, somewhat still, somewhat deep. But when we'd take the boat out on Lake Murray, we were the same. We were misfits, unguided, unbroken. We were brothers—amateur anglers with a loaded cooler and a headful of punk. We were alive. No bosses. No shitty wives. Just two lost boys who didn't want to be found.

Lake Murray is just as much a part of my DNA as the dust I grew up on. We swam it. We floated in it the best we could. We drank it. That lake was all we had, and it held whatever we could throw in it. Lake Murray covers about 50,000 acres, with a shoreline that runs about 500 miles. It is fed by the Saluda River, and like most places fed by rivers, the whole damn place is haunted. When the dam was finished and they flooded the area back in the '30s, the water came quick. Houses were moved, cemetery markers, etc., but there were several communities just swallowed up. The entire town of Countsville was flooded over. Cemeteries from family plots to slave graves were flooded too. And like a good horror story, they moved the markers but not the bodies. Go to the lake at night, either on it or in it, and you will feel them there.

Even though the town of Lexington predates Lake Murray, there is no doubt that the lake saved it. For a long time, the lake was a well-guarded secret by the locals. But soon enough, Lexington became a stopping place for out-of-towners to gas up on their way to the water. There was little here, just a small town and a big lake. The town didn't stand a chance. The lake won. Soon enough, out-of-towners stayed. The chains moved in. Soon enough, a Walmart, a K-Mart, a PetSmart, a Stein Mart. By the time Glen moved here, much of Lexington had grown and was growing still. I had already spent countless evenings on the lake gigging and bow fishing in the coves for gar. I had pulled out more bluegills and shellcrackers and channel cats and crappies and rockfish than I ever cared to remember. But back in those days we ate what we caught because it wasn't like there was a store to carry it or restaurant to serve it, and the idea of catch and release seemed about as stupid as anyone who ever said that a bad day fishing was better than a good day working.

Lexington was a different place back then, but it learned to grow with the lake and give itself over to murky-ass water. And soon enough the quiet coves that were loaded with largemouth got busy. Houses moved in, dock structures that jutted from the shoreline moved in. Enormous watercrafts to pull children with big teeth around the dam towers moved in. That's the way it happens, because that's the way it always happens.

And it happens worse here in the Midlands. As soon as someone whispers *I wish we had a…*sooner or later that wish comes true, and everything around that wish is changed forever. That tiny gas station is now Pay-Less shoes. The old bait shop was where the parking lot went for the Super Walmart. Hite's Dairy Bar is now a Rite Aid. Then Pizza Delivery. Then cable TV. Then a new cinematic multi-plex. A Target. A Kohl's. A sit-down restaurant you see on TV.

By the time Glen moved here, much of Lexington had grown into one big pain in the ass traffic jam. And soon enough, two boys, caught in the swirl of boredom and sprawl and one-too-many goddamned churches, found a way to live. We didn't fish to survive. We didn't fish to win some tournament we set with nature. We fished to get away, to not sit straight, to forget that just past the shore and the line of trees was a vanilla town full of vanilla do-gooders and nosey-types and fuck-heads who carry clipboards during their shift at the grocery store. We fished, simply put, because it was the best drug we could afford at the time.

Like a lot of kids in the South, we breathed through the stories we were told. When you are young, you yearn for those stories, those talks. But soon enough, men stop talking and start telling. Fathers tell sons. Bosses tell workers. Preachers tell congregations. The situation depends on one set being dumber than the other, hence one set being told by the other. In Lexington, it was hard to tell which set was which. Not because of the place or proximity of powerlines or the water table being fucked, but because our generation got smarter than anyone thought or ever gave us credit for. We educated ourselves by doing, if not by some initial guidance, by trial and error. We learn from our errors (or we're stupid). And like a lot of kids in the South, Glen and I had piled up enough errors by our mid-twenties to last four lifetimes. And like a lot of kids in the South, we were bitter for it. Fuck grocery store music. Fuck managers and their timeclocks. Fuck preachers and their Sunday shopping hours. Fuck farmers and the shit they spread. Fuck the hold-over debutantes and the shit they spread. Fuck old men who ask if the clerk knows the difference between paper and plastic. Fuck their wives for just standing there. And just when the day was about all we could pack into the last smoke break, one of us would say that we need to go fishing, and the other would say, fuck fishing.

We weren't fishermen. We didn't call it fishing or therapy or church as that would have been dishonest to our nihilistic ethos. Besides, the rednecks at work would have wanted to come and bring their dad's Crestliner with their dad's thirteen-inch depth-finder, and all the bull-shit they would swear by. We just wanted to catch fish and let them go, but to be ourselves in the process—Glen with his blue hair and me with a bright red nest of spikes. But the truth is, it *was* therapy. It *was* church.

Everything in our lives was about negotiating what we had control over and what we didn't. It seemed more fell in the latter category than anything else, no matter what we put into it. No matter how hard we worked at our jobs, no matter how much education I had received so far, no matter how much we tried to do things right by our wives, parents, and the general public, we were fuckups. We had all the potential in the world (we heard this often), but just refused to get with the program. So, we waved at boats that went by. Sometimes they waved back. Most of the time they just stared. No one ever stopped for directions. No one ever came up to us in a cove to ask what was biting. And as typical as that may sound, it was wonderful. It was just us and the water and whatever swam beneath it. The fact of the matter was that we needed the fish, and they didn't need us. We needed the release and it was only fair to do the same. Besides we'd have the rest of our lives to prove ourselves right into middle management. Here we could just be high and fish, and if we caught anything, great, and if we didn't, we didn't care.

We listened to each other and learned from each other. Glen taught me how to tie swivels and set the weight, when to use crickets, when to use shad, when to use jerkbaits or crankbaits or spinners. I taught him all the poets I knew and pointed out the gulls. Just two boys talking shit about this or that and usually concluding with the only possible metric that made sense or didn't. And when the fish weren't biting, we moved on to the next cove. Depending on the time of day, maybe the big water. And we drank. And we got high. And if we caught anything, we gave it back. Fishing was simple. Fishing was good living. There was nothing redneck about it.

Like a lot of kids in the South, Glen and I should have been diagnosed with attention deficit disorder. Like a lot of kids in the South, we wrestled with boredom and the impulsivity that comes from it. Like a lot of kids in the South, we both subscribed to self-medicating methods. On the shore, you could fill your days wandering around town, digging your tongue into your teeth. It wasn't about right or wrong, but about what was real and what was stupid. People trying too hard to follow in the footsteps they had no business stepping in. We were bored with it, laughed when the store manager approached us about going into the management program. Getting stoned and going fishing was about the realest thing we did.

There were no cathartic experiences that I can recall at that time, but it was probably the calmest my mind had ever been. There were times when the wind is just enough to tickle the top of the water, and the sun, with no competition for cover, would reflect and shimmer, and we saw what heaven looks like. There were times when the breeze made the pine needles dance to the music we played in our heads, and we were the hands of God reaching down, whether too shallow or too deep, to pluck whatever was dumb enough to come near it. And then one of us would fart and there were times that may have been the only God we felt that day. There were times we set to cast out and make sound effects or pretend to be Bill Dance or Roland Martin and Glen would be the host and I would ask dumbass questions and sometimes a Game Warden with DNR would ride by slow and Glen would salute and I would waive and act like I caught Godzilla. There were times we got so high we just sat in the boat and drifted around an island. Even now, when my mind starts racing with ideas and I am haunted by images, I still go back to the sound of the water's chop against the boat and the rhythm of the reel like they were a part of God's lullaby for guys who work hard and deserve the rest. There were times I hummed an old hymn as I'd cup a crappie back into the water.

I couldn't have known then, but looking back, much of what I understand about writing was shaped from fishing. I'm sure that early on in my career, I landed a publication much like I first fished. I threw something in and got lucky. But given time, learning the value of measure and control, I learned that you have to work at anything that is worth a return. And sometimes, I can work as hard as I know to work and still end up with an empty hook. Much like writing. Forget who plays the fisher and who plays the fish. It's simply about the time we give and the time we take, doing and redoing again, and most importantly there will be a factor you have no control over. Some guys can piss off the side of a boat. Some guys can't. Some have time. Some don't.

Time has a way of getting away from us when we are fishing. Yet, time has a way of standing still when we are fishing. Time is a slippery fish. Time is an asshole. A collective of what we did or didn't do. What we said or didn't say, especially when we had the chance or didn't. That's what I have to write about now. But then, I needed to fish. Because somewhere in the quiet, somewhere in the haze when the morning falls to the sun, two boys who had, for the most part waded through a fair amount of shit, smiled back. I learned more about who I am and what I am doing now because I fished then. Because I fished with Glen. And even still, too many moments in silence, doing nothing, when we could have been fishing—fishing for something different, original, alive.

Like a lot of kids in the South, I couldn't help but repeat what I had always heard. Like the time a gull shit on Glen's back. I told him that it was good luck and tossed him a towel. We didn't fish much after that. Soon enough, I had a son. Soon enough, he had a daughter. I went to graduate school and started teaching. Glen went to work as a welder for an industrial pipe fabricator in the Upstate. Because that's what happens. That's what always happens. Wishing has nothing to do with it. We grow. We roll. We roll on. That's the life of a lake. That's what fish have to think. That's certainly life just past the banks. Until it isn't.

When Ryan (Glen's brother) called me to tell me that Glen had been killed at work, how a chain hoisting industrial piping broke, he used words like *blunt force trauma* and *accident*. I kept going back to the last time I saw Glen, how it couldn't have been more than a month, just two guys going in opposite directions passing each other at a gas station. We spoke a bit and let the current pull us out. I think I even said over my shoulder that we should go do some fishing, but he was already in the door and didn't hear me. Life is just like that—we swim through the daily grime one minute, and soon enough we're yanked away and gone forever.

In the casket, Glen, with his seed cap and sunglasses and pack of cigarettes in his hands against his chest, looked like he could've been waiting for the next big bite. *That's how he would've wanted it,* they said. *That would've been his wish.* He was twenty-seven years old. If I had the chance to make wishes come true, I'd like to keep it simple. I'd wish more than anything that Ryan didn't call me that night. I'd wish more than anything that everyone takes the time to give back what is given. I'd wish more than anything someone would ask me if I wanted to go fishing, just so I could say fuck fishing.

Sucker

JIM MINICK

We pause on the pasture shoals before wading in. Red Creek is fifteen feet wide with shallows, riffles, and deep holes, crayfish, minnows, and—this time of year—suckers. When we step in, our bare calves grow numb in the cold. We push upstream, clouds of silt drifting behind like the late-spring clouds above. My best friend Joe works the left bank, I the right, pitchforks ready, tines shining.

The first big hole bottoms before us under the butcher shop foundation. My grandfather told me of days when blood poured out of the floor drain to drop twenty feet into the water, thus giving the creek its name.

No structure looms above us now, just a huge concrete base covered by honeysuckle with that one-eyed drain peering out.

I poke under the foundation and a dark flash of fish shoots out. Joe sees it too late, throws behind, misses. "Ahead on the right," I yell, and Joe nods. The sucker disappears under the bridge. We wade into its shadow.

The creek narrows to one side, leaving a wide swath of gravel and sand under most of the bridge, making this our best hide-out, the place where we get away from parents, and Newburg, and the rest of this Pennsylvania countryside. Like back in the winter, we're pelting traffic with ice balls and one car suddenly stops, the brake lights turning to reverse lights as the car veers closer, the driver's angry sneer becoming visible as he looks over the rear seat. And off we go, running in different directions, me toward the post office, Joe around the church, all of the paths circling back to under this bridge where we gather, catch our breath, laugh, and take turns poking a head out, waiting, hoping that sucker of a mad driver has gone.

Joe sees this sucker of a fish holding steady in the current, just in the edge of sunlight. I wait as Joe inches forward, arches back, and throws. The fork finds flesh and our whoops echo off the underside of the bridge. The first fish of the morning, and the stringer no longer jangles.

To state the obvious: A sucker is a sucker because of its mouth. Instead of facing forward, like most fish mouths, a sucker's mouth faces the bottom, in line with the rest of its flat-bellied body. Its Latin name, Catostomidae, has the Greek roots of *kata*, meaning "down," and *stoma*, meaning "mouth," and this "down-mouth" has large, fleshy lips so it can more easily suck up bits of food off the creek's bottom.

A foot or so in length, suckers weigh one to three pounds and can live for at least ten years. Males mature in two years, while females mature in three. The suckers we gig have olive-colored backs, white bellies, and sides that shimmer like just polished silver and brass.

An old photograph of my grandparents after their wedding: They're at a cabin in the mountains, some place I don't recognize, and between them they hold a long stringer of fish, a dozen or so trout. The stringer curves with the weight; it mirrors their smiles.

They both loved to fish, and they often took me with them—to Possum Lake, or way up in the mountains to Phoenix Mill, a small stream lined by hemlocks where years later I'd get married. Most of the fishing my grandparents and I did, though, was at the farm pond, a half-acre circle nested into the folds of the fields, out of sight of house and barns. Because Grandma had arthritis and Grandpa emphysema, we didn't walk the half-mile lane. Sometimes we drove the Buick, but usually, Grandpa started the Cub tractor and Grandma and I rode in the small wagon, our fishing rods jangling over each rut.

At the pond, we set out lawn chairs and lit punk sticks to keep the gnats away. My grandparents taught me to bait my hook with worms from the garden or kernels of corn or bread rolled into a ball. The bobbers bounced on the water's surface, the rings of waves disappearing like the fish at that sudden intrusion. But not for long. These were bluegills, all sizes, some smaller than a Mason jar lid, others bigger than Grandpa's hand. One year, the bluegills were so thick they came to the water's edge and waited for the baited hook. They even struck unbaited hooks. Grandpa got so disgusted, he said to put all we caught in the bucket, not to throw any back, not even the smallest. He planned to eat the biggest and feed the rest to the barn cats. We caught at least thirty before heading in to help with the milking. At first, the cats didn't know what to do with the floundering fish, but soon the older ones chomped through the bluegills' bodies, while the kittens batted them in play.

In spring, suckers fin their way upstream. The males arrive first to claim the best shallows for spawning, and then they wait. When a female arrives, the males approach, sometimes as many as ten, but usually just one or two. They rub against her sides, she releases her eggs, and they immediately release their milt. The whole act takes only a few seconds. Then the female moves on in search of other males.

Both sexes "home." They know where they hatched and return to this native ground. Often they do so within the same few days of every year. Maybe they have homecoming reunions like we do on the Fourth of July.

I didn't get bored fishing as a kid, not at first, anyway. But when my grandparents and I caught so many bluegills we couldn't see the bottom of the bucket, or more often, when we caught so few and the bucket remained empty and the long moments of anticipation turned to long moments of staring at that blank water, waiting for the bobber to bob, then I'd wander the bank, trying different spots, getting my line caught. My grandparents just watched the water, sometimes talking, but mostly not. They didn't seem to mind when I gave them my rod so I could explore the woods.

I don't easily get bored, even now as an adult—except when I fish. I know the great pleasure friends find in casting and waiting and doing nothing more. I know the great peace of meditating, of being close to a body of water, and of securing your own food. I find those benefits often when I hunt deer, but I haven't found the same with a rod in hand.

There's a certain inefficiency with that comparison that I can't ignore. In a tree-stand I might sit and wait and come up empty for the same amount of time, but when I kill a deer, the freezer fills. Three or four deer, and the freezer's full for the year. Three or four bluegill or bass and you might have a few meals. They taste fine, especially the bluegill, but the larder remains empty.

Am I a sucker for not enjoying fishing? Probably so.

In the course of one spawning season, a female sucker can lay anywhere from 20,000 to 130,000 eggs. These eggs and young are left to live or die on their own. They take roughly twenty days to hatch and then about a month later, they migrate downstream, usually at night to avoid predators. From egg to this first migration, sometimes only three percent survive.

A sucker does not at first hatch with a sucker mouth. For its first few weeks, it feeds on the water surface. Then slowly, the mouth moves down the face and the fish becomes a bottom feeder. What evolutionary gain does this give the species to not at first be born with a *kata-stoma*? Scientists have guesses, but don't really know.

Ahead, a huge walnut shades the water, its roots hiding the next dark hole. Joe wades into the pool, while I circle wide to wait upstream.

This is the same tree that my dad and uncle Don gigged when they too were boys. Except then, on a dare, my uncle noodled this crevice. He leaned his fork against the bank and slowly slipped into the hole—inching forward, kneeling on the shaley bottom, his shoulders submerged, only his head above water. He worked his hands up under the roots. He felt rough wood, muddy bank, and then, the slick sides of what he wanted. In one quick flurry of hands and splashes, Uncle Don lunged and caught that slick-sided creature by the tail and pulled it out. But it felt different—skinnier. The long cord of muscle swiveled and lashed until Uncle Don finally saw the whole of it, no bottom-sucking snout-mouthed sucker, but a water snake whipping angry and striking bare skin. It swam away fast downstream.

Joe works his fork under the roots, but we see no snakes. Instead we both yell, "There," at the black flash. I arch and throw and my fork skips off the rocky bottom, the fish moving on upstream. I curse, retrieve the pitchfork, and we slog on. We have over three miles of stream before we reach Uncle Oscar Franklin's, who gladly takes any suckers we catch.

White suckers are what we gig, but they aren't the only suckers. A list of just a few includes: chubsucker (creek and lake), hog sucker (northern and Roanoke), rustyside sucker, torrent sucker, suckermouth minnow, and—oddly—harelip sucker.

A different suckerfish, known as remora, swims in oceans. They don't, however, have sucker mouths. Instead, they've evolved a suctioning fin that allows them to attach to larger creatures like turtles, sharks, and whales. What better way to not get eaten then by swimming under the belly of a shark.

For over sixty years, the citizens of Nixa, Missouri have held an annual Sucker Day. Each spring, they catch thousands of pounds of suckers to fry and feed to thousands of people. But they don't catch suckers with hook and bait, and they don't gig either. They grab. When the suckers are migrating upriver, Nixa citizens go to the streams with bait-less hooks. The sucker swims in sight, the fisher casts nearby, and when the fish swims close to the line, the fisher "grabs" it with the hook—anywhere on the fish's body—and reels it in.

The Sucker Day Festival officially starts with a parade on Friday evening. Then Saturday, Main Street is packed with vendors and guests. At noon, they feast and hand out awards: for the biggest caught (4 pounds); smallest (1 oz, 1 gram); the most caught (51); and, my favorite, the river with the best tasting suckers. They also crown a Sucker Queen and a Sucker King, high school students winning scholarships from the proceeds of the Sucker Day.

To be a sucker is to be had, an easy mark, a gullible fool, or as the *Oxford English Dictionary* defines it, a greenhorn, a simpleton.

Oh, the many times I've been a sucker. Like the time as a budding poet, still in my teens, I shared some of my writing with a new pastor, and he laughed.

Or the third time I had sex, or almost had it. I had driven all the way from Pennsylvania to North Carolina in a friend's Ford Pinto, just for this girl, a high school-turned-college sweetheart, a year older and down south for a summer internship. And there I was, horny and inside of her, when she said, "I think you should know I'm seeing someone else." That sucker-punch withered me up and shut me down faster than any sucker swimming from a gigging fork.

And now as a fifty-something with an ideal teaching job, I still feel like a sucker. I have two graduate degrees and thirty years of teaching, most of it enjoyable, but all of it chasing what more and more seems like an American Nightmare of pursuing the security of a steady paycheck and health insurance over chasing riskier dreams.

Maybe I was noodled a long time ago and only now begin to feel the hand that slowly squeezes me. Maybe if I quit this job, I'd be gigged by the high cost of health insurance or a medical disaster. As a snake or sucker, in this light, it doesn't look good.

A half mile from where we started, Joe and I approach the section of Red Creek we know best. Over the high bank, we can see the white bricks of his house a hundred yards away, the basketball goal and sloping backyard. We pause on our island and admire our carved set of stairs that ascend the steep bank. We use those steps every time we need to escape, treading on stones from shore to island to shore, walking the opposite bank a quarter mile till we reach the fence line of my grandparents' farm. There, at a huge-canopied white oak, we climb the crossover and hike through alfalfa, shooting groundhogs with our .22s.

But this island is our refuge. If we duck down and sit on our heels, no one can see us. We've caught crawfish here, corralled them into a pool until we had enough to boil in a tin can on a small fire that got us in trouble. We've dug clay from the bank to form fine sculptures, a toilet we both initiated and a nude woman that washed away in the next rain.

And there, just upstream from the island, a sucker works the pebbled bottom, unaware of my slow steps. I keep my shadow in the trees' shadows, and when I'm close, I lunge, release the fork, and finally hear not the water-muffled sound of metal on rocky bottom, but instead the thunk of flesh.

I hold the sucker to the sun. Light glistens off its silver and brassy scales, the black eyes seem clownishly large, and the fins are cloudy gray. I whoop and add it to the stringer. Then we move on.

Joe and I have known each other since before we could talk. We're distant cousins, and though he's just two months older, he often seems like two years older. He taught me how to gig, he shot a deer first, he drank and used tobacco and had sex first. And before all of this, he taught me about honeysuckle. How to pluck a bloom, nip the green base, and slowly pull the stamen backward through the flower to get its drop of "honey." We sampled different bushes, perfecting our technique, always finding a sweeter flower.

The best way to see a sucker is by his shadow. The shading of his scales blends with the silt and shale. You might see the tail flick as he shifts to face upstream, or you might see the dart as he zips into a root-bound hidey-hole. More likely, though, you'll see that oblong shadow wavering on the rocky bottom, a shadow that seems uncast until you make out that sleek body.

The best way for a sucker to see you is by your shadow or silhouette. Block the sun, and away she goes. Let your shadow cross over her, and bye-bye. Those eyes have evolved to their largeness because of you and the long history of other giggers—the herons and kingfishers and bob-cats and maybe even your great-great-grandmother.

The sucker is no sucker to the truth of light and shadow.

A sucker's mouth has no teeth like you'd expect. Instead, a single row lines its throat to grind food sucked from the stream floor. Suckers are omnivorous—bugs, snails, fish, plants—anything small enough to swallow.

Sometimes we gigged a female sucker still full of eggs. We pressed out the jelly-like orbs and watched them float downstream.

• • •

As we hike upstream in the late afternoon, our aim improves, our patience grows, and we spear more suckers, the stringer heavy with their weight. But we still miss more than we gig. Below Hensel's Hill, in a deep hole, we sit on the bank, feet in the water, to rest. If the hole was bigger, we could float on our backs, but the stream has narrowed, so we just sit.

"Don't move," Joe whispers. He slowly raises his fork, aiming for something I can't see. Then the grunt and thrust and yell as he waves his pitchfork in the air. But instead of a sucker, Joe's speared a giant crawfish, so big we have to guess-measure it without a tape. The blue- and red-tinted claws still move, so while Joe pins it to the ground, I use the digits of my finger to inch along its smooth shell. Eight inches, I say. Biggest we've ever seen, we both agree. If we had matches and a can, we'd roast it right there, but since we have neither, and the afternoon is waning, we leave it on the bank for some other creature to eat.

As the stream narrows even more, the brushy alders and dogwoods crowd in, so that we spend more time skirting the thickets than hunting fish. Eventually, the creek becomes a rivulet, and we call it a day. Six suckers hang from the stringer, and Uncle Oscar's house is in sight, a half mile away. We trudge through just-planted corn, cross the state road, climb his steep wooden steps, and knock. His round, bald head peers through the window. Uncle Oscar grins and invites us in, but we decline. He keeps his woodstove going most of the year, and the heat wafts out the door along with the smells of an old man who lives alone. We wait as he brings a pan, then Joe unhooks the suckers from the stringer, and we say goodbye and head home.

I always took other people's word about eating this fish. "Oh, it's all bone." "Nothing to it." "Not even worth heating up the skillet for."

I gigged several times, killing a dozen or so fish, but I never actually ate any suckers.

In suckerhood, not all is bad. I'm a sucker for the nip and run of dogs at play; for the family of five beavers damming a creek with trees we planted; for Bach and Mingus; for all birds, but especially ravens with their tumbling play-flight and pileated woodpeckers flashing black-and-white as they cackle into the woods. I'm a sucker for dark chocolate and fresh blueberries and raspberry jelly (but never the three together); for a student's good story to cover an excess of absences; for a good line of poetry to read over and over; for every turtle trying to cross every road; for blueberry canes in winter, red against snow. And I'm a sucker for the hazel of my wife's eyes, and the small curve of her earlobe, and for rich coves of woods we get lost in together.

The Encampment:
The Hotter, Younger Sister
C.J. BOX

When I die, I want my ashes spread in the Encampment River in Southern Wyoming.

Specifically, I'd like them scattered on the water near Commissary Park. That's where the forty-five-mile river enters Wyoming from its source near Buck Mountain in the Park Range in Northern Colorado.

The route taken by those ashes would include the fifteen miles of the Encampment Wilderness Area. They would flow through a deep canyon and pass under the gaze of bighorn sheep, elk, bears, moose, deer, river otters, mountain lions, and bald eagles. The ashes would sluice through river rocks in fast white-water and eventually slow down and emerge south of the small villages of Riverside and Encampment, where the run-off and spring water has joined the flow that there is enough volume early in the summer for rafts and drift boats. They'd pass my cabin on the bank of the river through a new river restoration project, then through private ranchland, then the ashes would serpentine through the public "state section" over the gaze of wild rainbow and brown trout. The ashes (if there were any left, so just stay with me here) would drift down through the Encampment River Canyon and finally pour into the North Platte River at a place called the Rainbow Hole (for very good reasons).

It would be a fine last trip.

Let's say that the Upper North Platte River, which is rightly famous for its scenery and great fishing, was your beautiful girlfriend. If so, the Encampment is her hotter and wilder younger sister. She is trouble with a capital "T".

Over the years, the Encampment has beaten me far more times than I've beaten it. The river is small, wild, challenging, and vindictive at times. While floating it, the oarsman has to be on top of his or her game *every single second* or the boat will get hung up on rocks or thrown into a tangle of downed timber.

Once on the river, anything can and will happen. I've been rained on, snowed on, blown upriver by the wind in the canyon, and had more than a few trips where we couldn't find a single willing trout.

Anglers will get one shot at a good-looking hole and the cast has to be perfect. While wading it, I've seen large brown trout practically shoot through the legs of my waders but refuse to take a fly. I've seen pods of large fish sipping Tricos under the protection of overhanging brush where an artificial fly can't reach them.

The river is small enough that it's horribly easy to get hung up on both front and back casts. And if you're in a boat and it happens, there is no other choice but to break it off. I've often thought it might just be easier at the beginning of the season to simply open my fly boxes and dump all the flies into the water and let the current wash them away. That way it would save me the time and trouble of losing each one individually over the coming months of frustration.

And then there's the mythical green drake hatch on the Encampment.

For thirty years, I've heard stories about it. Supposedly it was a magical period (usually occurring around the Fourth of July) where huge trout smack huge green drakes on the surface in a kind of drunken frenzy. When it occurs, fishing guides suddenly call in sick that day and businesses in Saratoga flip their open signs to "closed." And those who were on the river during the mythical hatch say they've never experienced anything quite like it.

I pursued the alleged green drake hatch year after year. I was on the water on July 4th and days preceding and following it. No green drakes. Inevitably, after I gave up and went home, I'd hear later I missed it by a day. It's kind of like arriving in an unfamiliar city during a storm where all the residents say, "Man, you should have been here *yesterday*."

Once, while floating the Encampment in the early summer, we rounded the last bend before the Rainbow Hole. It was cool and rainy, and mist rose from the water. There in front of us, blocking the entrance to the North Platte River, was one of the biggest bull moose I've ever seen in the wild.

It wasn't startled by our approach. In fact, it wouldn't move. We kept waiting for it to continue across the river.

We got close enough we could smell him and see beads of rain on his thick black hide. It wouldn't budge.

We managed to row just behind it, and while we did I recalled videos I'd seen of bull moose kicking the crap out of dumb tourists.

But because we were on the water, he perceived no threat from us. He let us pass by, and soon he was obscured by the mist.

The image of that bull moose standing in the Encampment will stay with me forever.

During our fishing trip last summer, I was wading knee-deep in the Encampment on a beautiful July morning. I'd caught and released a couple of small rainbows on dry flies, which had already made the day a success. But compared to the many large fish we'd hooked into on the North Platte the day before, it was nothing to write home (or an essay) about.

That's when I heard a big, sloppy *sploosh* behind me. Then another. I turned expecting to see that bull moose again—back to finish me off.

But it wasn't the moose.

There, on the surface of the water was what looked like an armada of tiny sailboats floating downstream. As I realized what was happening, a big brown hit one of the sailboats with a splash. Then the river came alive.

It was the mythical green drake hatch and I was in the middle of it.

My hands shook as I tied on a fly. The water boiled around me. The takes on the surface were percussive. I caught a sixteen-inch rainbow on my first cast, and a seventeen-inch brown on my second. The armada floated to me and continued on. I caught fish after fish. I even caught one on a clumsy back cast!

Then it was over. The convoy of green drakes had passed and the river went quiet again.

I stood on the bank shaking my head and waiting for my heartbeat to return to normal.

When I die, I want my ashes spread in the Encampment River.

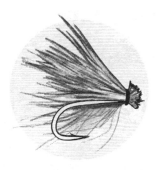

Temporal
TODD DAVIS

W ater has memory. It holds onto trace elements for decades. Sometimes centuries. Sometimes longer. Acid mine drainage. Oil spills. Simpler pollution, like sewage or fertilizer. Hard rains washing away soil from farm fields, planting silt in streams, a harvest of warming water that makes it impossible for speckled trout to survive.

We're made of water, too. Our birth rite. Our history and mother. We finned and wriggled through her. Crawled up a bank and out of her depths eons ago. So many millennia have passed that even evolution has a hard time remembering. Yet our bones and skin remember when we draw near to the sound of moving water. The slap of waves on sand and stone. Our heart and ears recalling that time floating in an amniotic sea.

I think part of catching a native trout along the Allegheny Front in central Pennsylvania is a connection to that species-memory, memorial etched on our DNA. In the quiet of the woods, near the music of a creek that makes the life of these fish possible, exists a bit of sacred evidence, a trace of history that suggests our long-ago making.

Ask an angler about the movement of a trout at the end of her line, the bending of the rod, the surge of power. Ask what it's like to hold a fish, muscled sides thrashing, tail and head twisting. Ask about the beauty of the fish. The wormy ovals. The colors draped in a cloak woven from exquisite flecks of gold. The faint amethyst of its scales. Ask. You'll be told—often in halting speech because language fails in moments like this—the life of that fish is somehow our life as well.

Peering into the clear water of a stream, seeing beneath its surface as fingerlings flit and scatter beneath stone or undercut banks, is akin to an originary desire. Recollection of that first loving darkness, buoyed, moving like slippery fish.

We live in an age that denies so much about the nature of our existence. Mostly we deny the body, the material, the temporal. Not so much in giving in to our carnal appetites—we've built entire industries around such fetishes—but in separating our bodies from our spirits, treating them as if we were simply renting. I think we'd do well to remember Jim Harrison's mantra, a line he borrowed from Shakespeare, that chides us for our willful forgetting: "We are nature, too."

And because we're nature, too, wildness is part of our inheritance. Try as we might, we can't separate ourselves from the elements, from the elemental. The wind in the crowns of trees. The astonishment when a bobcat pads across the snow's crust. The fear when a bear or moose moves through an alder swamp, so close we can smell the primacy of the world we share.

I suppose one reason I'm drawn to fly-fishing for brookies is the possibility of such revelation. And I ought to confess that I mean revelation in all its manifestations, in all its fierceness, all its mystically material forms.

I don't fish for brook trout with anything but dry flies. An elk hair caddis for the early part of spring. Maybe a blue-winged olive on the rare afternoon in late April. A parachute sulphur in May. After that a Royal Wulff works just fine until the spawn in November.

But I'm not a dry-fly purist. The fact is I don't believe a speckled trout would be disgraced if you nymphed for it or threaded a worm over a hook. The reason I fish for natives with dry flies alone is because I'm obsessed with the rise. Fixated on the manner in which these most exquisite fish reveal themselves to us. Divulging where in the pool or riffle they've been hiding. Suddenly privy to the secrets they've been keeping.

And each time a native materializes I'm sorely afraid, in the old-fashioned sense of that phrase. Sublime beauty leading to awe. A feeling comprised of both love and fear. Overpowered by the fact that I've done nothing to earn this revelation. Consumed by a dread that we will so despoil our streams and rivers that these trout might vanish forever.

On the second day of June, in a year of nearly daily rain that has kept the rivers and streams unseasonably cool, my son Noah and I climb the small creek to the west of our house along the Allegheny Front, the Little Juniata River too high to wade for wild browns. From past experience, we have a strong premonition that the larger fish may be looking up. Small mountain runs flushed white with oxygen. If you're a brook trout, this is a day to be a bit careless, ignoring heron and kingfisher, swimming with abandon and feeding with little restraint.

After fifteen years of living in the creases and folds of these mountains, we know the pools that normally run slow, too slow to host speckleds in summer's heat. But with this recent deluge—more than four inches of rain in the past three days—these same pools offer respite to fish whose constant struggles against the stronger currents have left them tired and hungry.

After missing a sizeable trout, back surging out of the water as it tried to chase the fly all the way to the end of the pool, Noah and I walk to the pond that settles between two sharply-rising ridges, ground scooped into a bowl of spring-fed water. The stream spills in at the southern end, then heads north to cascade over a small waterfall.

We approach on our knees, wary to spook the larger trout who patrol the pond's edges. Through newly formed spicebush leaves we spy a splash at the far end near a beaver den. Then a spatter. A splat. A smack. The normally-still pond, where brook trout reveal themselves with guarded sips, has collapsed into a cacophony of unselfconscious, even raucous, feeding that has little to do with the high water.

What does it mean to pay witness to something you've never seen before? I remember the first time I cut open a large brown trout's belly, looking forward to the dill and butter that would dress its pink and white flesh, only to find a half-digested mouse in its stomach, the myths that occasion the tying of mouse-flies suddenly realized.

And here, with the pond overwhelmed in ring after ring, ripples crashing into ripples, suggesting the ways the universe is concentric, connected, reshaped by our every movement, we watch the biggest trout in the pond gather themselves, committing to their cravings, using the swivel of their tails to thrust into the air where they can devour the insects that are hatching.

We've never seen this winged species in these mountains. Never dreamt or hoped that they existed here, in the privacy of this wood, because this fly demands the most unsullied of places, and over the past 150 years these woods have been clear cut and mined, every last cent wrung from their bones.

We watch, dumbstruck, as green drakes slither from their shucks, wriggling out of their former lives, to catch in an eddy. Some of them walking onto our legs and hands to dry their wings, which resemble the most ornate stain glass.

Noah holds one up to the light, only inches from his face. Life examining life, a gesture toward our wonder at being here, at existing at all. The intimacy of this act—witnessing the birth of a newly formed creature—slows and quiets us, despite those crashing fish. And so a father and son speak in hushed whispers, as if they've stumbled into a chapel, vespers already in progress.

We take pictures of the drakes in different stages. We try to describe the structure of the wings, the pleasing dark greens. I point to the pond's surface where the colors of the surrounding forest are reflected, starting with the bracken fern that edges up the hill. Then the sugar and red maples. And after that the rhododendron, beech, and hemlock. Every colored shade offering a difference—from lime and olive to pickle and seaweed.

Everywhere we look is an emerald prism of refraction and reflection. And these improbable, impossible flies, a gift rising into the air for a brief time. A temporal meeting, then a faltering. A falling back onto the green surface of the water where those speckled trout, whose own backs hold a variegation of mixed verdure, consume yet more green. Until the world seems like nothing but fecundity and death. A father and son smiling at each other. Not sure what comes next. But hoping it will begin with a fish.

Some Thoughts About Marriage Before I Wed

REBECCA GAYLE HOWELL

By one notion, Cleo rose in the Van Lear, Kentucky morning. He'd dress, shout something smart to Frankie as her goodbye, drive to the Druther's in Paintsville and drink his coffee with the boys, then leave it all behind for that day's make-or-break at Bob's Pay Lake. Cleo'd park a straight line into that gravel lot, then raise the hatch on his Chevette to take out the six gleaming shark poles he knew could work the only job he had, to hook Old 69, the resident mud cat, a fish as large as a lie no one believed. All the men put their dollars in that cat's jar, a good-sport Powerball for the one of them who would pull him up out of his loungey, bottom-feeding privacies, his forgotten holler I'm sure 69 preferred to be forgotten in.

I never knew Cleo. He was my love's daddy's daddy, a man who I've been told was gentle and kind, with enough violence in him to make Frankie laugh off her old life. Together, they were hoarders; between the wiles of *Time* magazines and electronic parts, paths cut through their home, making way to the necessaries. In Cleo's day Van Lear was a Consolidated town. He'd mined, briefly, as a scab, but his career was cards and liquor. He told his family he was a rich man, kept wads of money in his pocket, rolls of money, to show. The house sat on Silk Stocking Loop and presented itself like a boss's house, with a porch that rose to a second-story roof by way of four grand, vinyl-sided columns. Triumphant and drunk, Cleo would clean out the dress store for Frankie just to see her smile. Then he'd lose it all the next night; return her dresses in the day's light. Big was Cleo's style; I can see those shark poles dug into the beach's curve, a neat, strategic row, the sure future. "Mix up some biscuits and gravy, Frankie! I'm taking this boy fishing!" he'd say to the whole house, the whole town, if it would only listen.

The son of Cleo had a different style: bigger. Bigger shouting. Bigger praying. Harder hitting. A miner, exhausted from working his double shift, he fell asleep driving home one early morning, sent his truck end over end over end in an empty field. Paralyzed on one side of his body and for ten years more he terrorized his family. When his wife finally reached *her* courage, she left him, then he married another woman, and another.

My people prefer to be small. Grandaddy raised his family on Buckhorn, about a hundred miles from Cleo and Frankie, on an isolated few acres where he and my grandma toiled to feed their ten kids and the annual pig. He'd drank rotgut when he was young, but did not run it, as his brothers did. Instead he sobered into a silence and rolled his own.

"All your grandfather wanted was to be up in that holler with his family, where everybody else would leave him alone," my mother's repeated warning against—what?—not seeing the world, I suppose, which I have done, thanks entirely to my mother's leave-taking of that family when she was a girl.

She likes to fish, my mom. After she reached her courage and left my father, a boyfriend came around who sold fast cars and who showed up many a night at our door in a Corvette or a Firebird, soused and bullying; my mother shouting at me to call the police. On the good Saturdays, Kenneth would take her fishing, and sometimes we'd all congregate to fry what they'd caught, eat together, play cards together, until the sun fell. He was the only boyfriend, the risk my mom took. After she left him, for years after, we'd be at the doctor's office or the mall only to find upon our return another dead fish tied to the car's door handle. I often think about Frankie. She had "the sight," I'm told, ESP. She could see into the veil and tell what would soon happen, but she could not see her son for who he was, or her husband; or, she did and did not mind.

A pay lake is a dirty place. Shallow, stagnant waters teeming with old-growth fish meant for the wild rivers. Trophies, they call the flatheads and blues, most of them twenty years-old and big as me. As in, something you win. As in, yours. A catfish has no scales on her skin. She's fleshy and with those long whiskers; all of it, her whole body, a sensor that can smell and taste and hear by touch, by nearness. She'll spend her day in quiescence, under some rock, still, but alert; we'll say she's sleeping but we're wrong.

Before Pangea, all of Kentucky was algae; a promise secured under the sea. Today, we are landlocked. We fake our lakes and bury our head-streams. We import drinking water from Virginia. We don't know each other or each other's places or our own. The first time I ever was in Van Lear my love took me there. It was early days for our affair, snow still on the ground. We drove through rows of houses sheltering dealers and users, neighbors with cue balls for eyes, as well as the rows of tidy homes belonging to the Church of Christ faithful, the neighbors with a plan. Since 1945, since the war was won, Van Lear has been unincorporated; officially, it is an accident of buildings, an undetermined human population with no representation and no boundaries; a place that exists because of tradition. Because that's the way it's always been. Because we all got to have someone. As my love drove that cold day I watched out the window, wondering to God how any of us choose each other, if not by tradition. But that's another story worth believing only if you have a dollar in the jar.

Memory of Water
SILAS HOUSE

Sometimes the grief is so big that the remembering is unbearable. Nowadays, when I go back to Dale Hollow Lake, that's the trade-off: being flooded with the memories that fill me with equal parts joy and sorrow. As soon as I see its acorn-green waters I am all remembering. I jump out of my truck, rush down to the lake bank, and put my hands into the water. I pluck up some of the jagged rocks, run my fingers over them, skip them across the surface. Out yonder is the island where we camped every summer and fall, lush with cedars and tulip poplars. Before me is the wide stretch where the best bluegills nested in the weed-banks in early June, where we used to sit in the mists of early mornings, awaiting their bites. Over there is the holler where we fished in the hot evenings, seeking shade along with the sun grannies. All of the best memories of my childhood play out in flickering, grainy projections on the mountainsides crowding around the lake. Snapshots are scattered on the waters before me, bobbing on the small waves. I see the ones who have passed on, who taught me. I see the ones who are still with me, but old now. I see the ones who have gone their separate ways for one reason or another. Life is what we gain and what we lose. Life is those spaces between the joy and sorrow I feel every time I come back here, to my favorite place in the world.

They always told me we came from Native American royalty and Irish Republicans who nearly starved to death during the Famine. My family's stories and songs were carried here from the green pastures of Lancashire in Northern England, the icy winds of Northeast Scotland. I am not sure about the truth of our genealogy. What I do know is that for the past 100 years my family on both sides never had any money, and my mother's family most certainly did not.

The first one to rise up out of poverty, however, was my great-uncle, Dave Sizemore, who used his keen intelligence to make money hauling coal, working in garages, and in the mines once he returned from fighting in World War II. A few years before, a huge new lake had been built a couple hours away. Dale Hollow Lake straddled the state border between Kentucky and Tennessee. Nearly 30,000 acres of surface water with 620 miles of shoreline and stocked with a gracious plenty of bass, crappie, bluegill, catfish, walleye, muskie, and trout.

International news was made there right around the time my Uncle Dave had accrued enough savings to buy a little green johnboat.

On the morning of July 9, 1955, David Hayes, his wife, and their little boy were trolling the lake for smallmouth and walleye. They weren't getting many bites until they trolled up Illwill Creek, where the space between two swaying weedbeds produced a massive strike on David's Tru-Temper steel rod, outfitted with a Penn Peer 209 reel. He had about 300 feet of line of his 20-pound test line out and he wrestled to get the monster close enough to his boat to put a net under it. He later said he knew it was "a pretty good smallmouth" but had no inkling it might be a record setter. He put it in his cooler with plans to clean it later for eating. When he went to nearby Wisdom Dock, the home of a famous fishing camp at the time, he asked the marina attendant to weigh the bass while he filled up with gas. The fish lacked an ounce weighing twelve pounds. It was twenty-seven inches long with a girth of more than twenty-one inches.

Uncle Dave read about the world record catch in the newspaper and figured that even if he couldn't capture such a giant there was bound to be good fishing at Dale Hollow. And there was. He came home with reports of bluegill that bit so quickly he could barely keep up, of drum that pulled his boat up the cove while he was reeling them in, of a bass that broke his Shakespeare in two, leaving him with nothing but the reel half in hand as the other end swam away. He had evidence, too: beautiful white filets he had cleaned on the bank and put on ice to carry home. Not only that: his wife carried the film from his little Kodak down to Begley's Drugstore and had folks over to look at the pictures: Uncle Dave behind a stringer heavy with three dozen sun grannies and shell-crackers, Uncle Dave holding up a lovely golden-scaled walleye or a bulbous-eyed catfish.

But he had been moved by more than the fish. "The water is so clear there you can see plumb to the bottom way out in the middle," he exaggerated. "And it's water big as an ocean," he continued. "The biggest old cedar trees every whichaway you look." Uncle Dave leaned forward. "I tell you what, now—it's the prettiest place I ever seen in my life."

Like all the best storytellers he operated in hyperbole. But he was not that far off base. Dale Hollow Lake is a place of beauty that is hard to surpass. Its sunsets rival those of Key West. The woods there are different. Still. Fragrant with all of those cedars. Quiet but for the music birds and crickets make. And the water is incredibly clean, with large pastures of water wider than many lakes in the South.

By the early 1960s, my mother's side of the family was just beginning to work their way up out of hard poverty. Theirs is the same story as many Appalachian families of the 20th century: in the early 1900s they were self-sustaining farmers who saw their culture radically changed by the advent of the industrial revolution. They witnessed the shift between a barter and cash culture in the hills. They witnessed their people going from totally independent farmers to totally dependent sawyers and miners. They were briefly part of the Appalachian Diaspora: WWII and busts in the coal and timber industries led them north where they were either terribly miserable and returned immediately or found the money made there too good to refuse and stayed, perpetually homesick. All of my mother's family members only made jaunts into Ohio and Michigan long enough to get ahead and came rushing back down the Dixie Highway to claim any back-breaking job they could that would allow them to stay in the land they loved. They were waitresses, mechanics, miners, truck drivers, housecleaners. They were the working class people everyone looked down upon. But they worked hard and made a living and before they knew it, much to their surprise, they could even entertain the notion of going on a vacation. They didn't want to go far— no one in my family ventured to Myrtle Beach or anywhere on the coast until the late 1980s—but they did want to start enjoying this leisure time that Americans were talking about.

A fishing vacation sounded perfect. Led by a beaming Uncle Dave, they made the three-hour trek down to the state line and launched their little aluminum johnboats at Wisdom Dock. They made camp on one of the islands on the Kentucky side of the lake because they had a keen Commonwealth loyalty. They cooked huge meals there on Coleman stoves. They sat around the campfire at night and told big tales. The children spent the entire days swimming and roaming the woods.

They fished every morning and every evening.

I am picturing the woman who will become mother on one of those evenings. She is twenty-six, her great beauty in full bloom. It is June of 1971, standing on the slate bank of a small island with several canvas tents behind her. By now her family has been vacationing for at least a week every summer on Dale Hollow Lake for more than a decade and they have slowly accrued plenty of camping equipment. A gnat-smoke—a small pile of twigs and leaves that has been lit to produce a steady steam to combat insects—smolders nearby, sending an elongated grayish-white comma up into the cedar boughs. The air is soft and fragrant with the smell of millions of ripe summer leaves—green as limes—and the clean water supping at the edges of the island. Twilight is knitting itself into being over the western hills: red, purple, peach, pink. There is a particular kind of cool that comes down over a shaded place after a day that has been blazing hot. Only Southerners know this specific comfort. That's how the world felt that evening.

My future mother is watching the fishing boats return to shore. She is seven months pregnant with me, and she's enormous. The small aluminum johnboats are too precarious for her condition so she has stayed behind with only one ancient great-aunt, who has been snoring softly in a metal lawn chair the entire time, while everyone else went out to fish. For the past two hours she has napped, read *Ladies' Home Journal*, built the gnat smoke, roamed the tiny island and memorized its ferns, its rocks, its small sounds. And now she is looking out on everyone she loves in the whole world: her husband, her sister, both her brothers, all of her uncles and aunts, sisters-in-law and brother-in-law, nieces and nephews, cousins. Her hand rests on her large belly, which possesses what she loves the most, and will love the most for the rest of her life: me.

"Who caught the biggest one?" she calls out to them and they all answer at once, a clamor of joy, the children reaching for the silver stringer where the sunfish and crappie have been latched through the gills. Uncle Dave stands up and holds his hands three feet apart—exaggerating, as always. "Honey, I caught one with eyes like a calf!" he calls out and all of their laughter glides just above the water, rising up to her, sliding past and going into the coves and hollows beyond, up into the shadiest places.

Even in utero, I must have sensed how happy they all were. Maybe that's why I have always loved it so much. They were happy because they were all together.

This would become a family story that would be repeated many times and that phrase has been repeated on many family fishing trips since. Anytime someone caught a big fish they'd proclaim it to have eyes like a calf and that would lead to a discussion of Uncle Dave, who was among our family's best storytellers. For my family, the story was always the thing. The story was the point of anything one did. And of course fishing stories are among the best kind.

Snapshot:

About six years after my mother stood on that lake bank and laughed with her family floating on the water before her, I would be in a johnboat with my aunt, Sis, and my first cousin, Eleshia. Sis was the consummate fisherwoman in our family. Everyone said she had the magic touch but the main thing she possessed that so many men in our family didn't was enough patience to await the best strikes. I liked to go out fishing with her not only because I worshipped her but also because fishing with her was completely stress-free. The men were all good-natured in their competitiveness, but they were incredibly competitive nonetheless. So competitive, in fact, that they took the fun out of it for me. I couldn't stand the tension that arose in boats when they thought they were being out-fished by a brother-in-law or uncle. Nor did I enjoy the braggadocio in which so many men in my culture delighted. My father grew impatient with my lack of skill and couldn't sit still, pulling up anchor no sooner than we had gotten settled in a fishing hole. My uncle conjured too much competition between me and his son, who was always a better fisherman than me, and I couldn't enjoy it. On Sis's boat fishing was about relaxing and loving the lake. It was about listening to the water. Watching a heron who was doing his own fishing across the cove, his startling white form stalking the shallows.

I have a picture of that evening I am remembering. Someone—probably my parents—must have been momentarily parked nearby us long enough to snap the picture on an Instamatic. In the picture I am reeling in a good-sized bluegill and Sis is reaching forward to grab hold of the line before the fish gets off the hook. I am wearing a bright orange life vest and she has a blue kerchief over her black hair. The center of the picture is her hand—the round veins, the deeply tanned skin that revealed her Cherokee and Black Irish ancestry, the nails painted red, the hard work of waitressing apparent in her large knuckles. I always loved looking at her hands because they told as many stories as she did.

In those days she was a force. And all of the men in my family knew she could bring in more fish than them even though she did things completely differently than they did. Whereas they sat whispering to one another while they trolled until they came upon a happening spot, Sis had a magical knack for picking a fishing hole. She eyed the water, considered the day's weather, the time of year, and picked a place without discussing it with anyone else. There she would drop anchor and would not move until she had given the spot a good hour or so to produce strikes. During that time she leaned back in the boat with her reel in one hand and a Winston Light in the other, smoking and telling one story after another, interrupting her tales only to give me careful instruction. The men in my family tended to be more in the joking camp when it came to fishing directives—"You ain't holding ye mouth right, buddy, or you'd be getting more bites"—Sis calmly and firmly told me what to do:

No sir, now, you have to bait your own hook. *That's what makes you a fisherman.*

A stern look on her face that let me know she was proud of me for trying.

See there? Make sure your worm is on there good. Put that hook right through him as many times as you can.

She had no time for squeamishness. That was foolish talk.

Now don't let slack get in ye line.

Cigarette clamped between her teeth, one eye closed against the rising smoke.

No, honey, reel it in slow—real real slow.

Her hands atop mine, thumb and forefinger on the little black knobs of the handle of my Zebco 33.

When it bites you'll feel it in the center of your wrist.

A tap on the center of my wrist with her forefinger.

Watch the end of your rod.

A nod toward the end of my fishing pole.

You've got one, Little Man! Reel the fire out of it! Bring it in, bring it in, bring it—

I wish I could have back that time and all those times I sat on the water with her. I would listen more closely to her stories. I would close my eyes and savor every word. But having written that, I know that I did, back then. Like I said, I worshipped her, and that's what little country boys do with their good aunts and uncles: listen to every word, remember it all.

Often I did go out fishing with my parents, of course, and those were some of the only times we were all still together when I was a child. My parents were always in motion. They had both been raised poor— my mother was orphaned at nine, and my father was raised by a single mother who had to bring up nine children on her own after my paternal grandfather died when my daddy was five—and they had no intention of ever being poor again. So, they hardly ever stopped working. When I was very small my father was a well-known mechanic at the Shell station in London, Kentucky, right by the brand new interstate 75 that was kept busy by Yankees going to the Smoky Mountains or victims of the Appalachian Diaspora returning home for the weekend. He also poured concrete for the driveways of folks who could afford it in our little town. Later he kept up the concrete side-work when he became a supervisor at a fiberglass factory. My mother waitressed, worked in a refrigerator plant, and eventually took a job in the cafeteria where I went to elementary school, moving up to cashier and working there until I was out of high school. Once they were home the labors didn't cease: my mother kept an immaculate house and my father kept an immaculate yard. They always found something to do. At Dale Hollow they both sometimes struggled with the stillness. But they both loved to fish. Those were different times, when parents didn't feel the need to constantly be with their children. And my parents, being strict Pentecostals, did not take me to movies, carnivals, or even trick-or-treating. That always fell to Sis or my cousin, Eleshia. Even then I knew that our time out on the lake was special because it was the rare respite from work, the only time besides meals that the three of us spent any real amount of time being still together.

My father believed in near-silence while fishing. "Hush now, you're scare them off," he'd tell me. He liked to use crickets and I had more of an issue with putting the barb of the hook through the little notch on their underside than I did with repeatedly stabbing the slimy worms. I had always been taught that it was not only bad luck but also wrong to kill a cricket. Yet here we were slaughtering them for the sake of reeling in a fish. "It's different when you're doing it to get food," my daddy said.

Of course they told stories, too, while we were out on the water. We were a storytelling people. Not even the desire for silence could stop us. On my father's boat the stories were whispered but told nonetheless, and I think that I learned more about my parents while we were out fishing in the soft mornings and muggy evenings than any other time. I can see them, now, so plainly. Younger than I am now. The joy on my mother's face when she reeled in that massive drum that would become legendary in our family—"Boys I've caught me one with eyes like a calf this time!" The concentration on my father's face as he awaited a good strike. "I'm not good at waiting because I had to wait so much in the Army," he said, his face growing dark with his memories of being in Vietnam. He had had to wait in line at the mess hall. He had had to wait all night for the command to move forward, lying in the water of a rice field while snakes slithered by. Once he had to wait a week before taking his boots off. Now his feet were gnarled because of other weeks like that. He told me these stories only on the still waters of Dale Hollow Lake.

As if from a far, hovering distance, I see the three of us heading back to camp with our cooler full of fish on a misty morning. I see the white line our boat cuts on the water, the sway of the sandbar willow leaves when the small waves reach them from our wake. I see me in my little orange life vest, looking out at Dale Hollow Lake as if it was the whole future lain out before me. I see my young parents, how beautiful they were, how strong.

When I was a teenager I began to run with my Uncle Sam and his son, Terry, more often. Sam loved to drink and he allowed us to, as well. We could also cuss in front of him, so long as we didn't get too crazy with our language. By the time we were about seventeen he didn't even make us hide our smoking. We could completely be our teenaged selves with Uncle Sam.

By this time my family had started spending more than three weeks a year on the lake. A full ten days in June, a long weekend at Labor Day, and always a jaunt in the very early spring when the trout were biting. Uncle Sam loved fishing for trout in particular. He thought they were beautiful to behold, and they were. But they were hell to clean. And Terry and I had to do all of the cleaning.

Once we came in off the water all of the men—about a dozen of us— would gather on the bank to clean the fish. Another uncle, Doug, taught us how to filet, and we really thought we were something once we were able to produce two perfect slabs of shining white meat to slide into Ziploc bags. Most of the fish would be fried up in a big fish fry that would happen on the last night of our trip. Anything that was left over was taken home and frozen to be fried up for a huge family gathering later.

I never felt more like I fit in with the rest of the men in the family than when we were cleaning fish. I was not good at most of the things the men in my family did. I was a complete disaster at hunting and they never let me live down the fact that once when Uncle Sam took me squirrel hunting and left me alone by a massive beech to scope out my own kills he came back an hour later to find me propped against the tree, reading a ragged paperback I had brought along with me, shoved down into one of the large pockets of the too-big camos he had loaned me. I frowned at machismo, which my uncles and cousins delighted in—everything was a competition, everything was teasing, everything went back to talking about how good we were at fishing or hunting or getting the ladies. I was not the best at any of those things and the latter two held little to no interest for me at all. But I could clean fish as good as any of the rest of them.

There are lots of pictures of us cleaning the fish. Here's one:

We're all gathered around the table where we've cleaned dozens of fish on two rectangular cutting boards and with two metal dish pans— one for guts and scales, one for fresh water to wash the filets. I'm about eighteen, my face still plumb with promise and youth. A University of Kentucky cap sits awkwardly atop my head. I have a thin, unfortunate moustache. I'm wearing my Tom Petty *Full Moon Fever* t-shirt, which I wore so much that year that it fell apart in the washer one day. All around me are the men of my family. My cousin Terry has his arm crooked around my neck and is pulling me in toward him. We have on the same shirt as we've bought it at the same concert. We do everything together. Another cousin, John Paul, is leaning against me. My uncles are all in uproarious laughter. One of them has said something disparaging or vulgar about the other one. My Uncle Doug is giving Uncle Sam rabbit ears. My father is looking at me. In the picture, I belong.

Much has changed over the last couple of decades for my family. First, Uncle Dave, the man responsible for all of our times on Dale Hollow Lake, died in 1996. With him went a universe of stories, but I preserved many of them; a slightly fictionalized version of him and his tales are at the heart of my first novel. Several other of the older ones passed on as well and with each of them went thousands of memories and jokes and knowledge.

By the mid 1990s my parents, uncles, and aunts had tired of island camping, which involves a tremendous amount of work, especially for people who insist on cooking full meals of green beans, fried chicken, mashed potatoes, homemade biscuits, bulldog gravy, and the like instead of simply nibbling on sandwiches and canned food like most campers would. Many of them bought RVs and we relocated to a tame campground across the lake that sits right at the water's edge. Instead of bathing in the lake and going into the woods to use the toilet we were now made more civilized—and less fun—by the conveniences of three shower houses being at our disposal. I refused to sleep in an air-conditioned motor home and continued to camp in a tent so I could hear the whippoorwills at night. Not being on the island anymore changed how much we were all together every minute of the day. But each day we awoke to the lake at our doorstep. Each day the boats went out at sunrise and an hour before sunset. Each day the men gathered to clean the fish.

Everyone is older now. They need more rest. Sometimes my father doesn't feel like going out to fish anymore. His back hurts too much. His body aches from Vietnam and hard work and old age. They all want to cook less large meals but everyone is still ready to work when it comes to fish fry night. Nobody is about to let that tradition die.

Worst of all, hardest of all, we lost my Aunt Sis and my Uncle Sam in the space of one month in 2015. She was 79 and he was 74. Always, when I think of them, I see them on Dale Hollow Lake, out fishing. The evening sun lighting their faces with a golden glow, their laughter carrying across the water, their stories as we sat around the campfire at night. Always, I remember them there, on the lake they loved, doing what they loved most of all—camping, fishing, telling stories, being together.

All these memories connected to one lake, to fishing. How does one go forward loving the place and the thing when they bloom up such grieving? Because the grieving is the loving.

The first time we went back to the lake after their passings was just about the hardest thing I've ever done. But also the most necessary. And each time I've been back it's been just as hard. But I must keep going because they cannot. And because I feel them there more than anywhere else. Especially when I'm out on the boat with a fishing pole in my hand. Especially when there is that little tap in the middle of my wrist and I perk up to begin bringing it into the boat.

CONTRIBUTORS

David Joy is the author of the Edgar nominated novel *Where All Light Tends To Go*, as well as the novels *The Weight Of This World* and *The Line That Held Us*. His memoir, *Growing Gills: A Fly Fisherman's Journey*, was a finalist for the Reed Environmental Writing Award and the Ragan Old North State Award for Nonfiction. His latest stories and essays have appeared in *Time*, *The New York Times Magazine*, *Garden & Gun*, and *The Bitter Southerner*. He lives in Jackson County, North Carolina.

Taylor Brown grew up on the Georgia coast. His fiction has appeared in more than twenty publications including *The Baltimore Review*, *The North Carolina Literary Review*, and *storySouth*. His short story collection *In the Season of Blood and Gold* was a finalist in the short story category of the 2015 International Book Awards. He is the author of three novels: *Fallen Land*, *The River Of Kings*, and *Gods Of Howl Mountain*. An Eagle Scout, he lives in Wilmington, North Carolina.

J.C. Sasser started her professional career at age 12, working as a dishwasher, waitress, and cook at a truck stop off Georgia's I-16. Over her life, she has worked as an envelope licker, tortoise tagger, lifeguard, Senate page, model, editor, water-polo coach, marine biologist, plant grower, software consultant, and 6-Sigma Black Belt. She is the author of the novel *Gradle Bird*. Sasser lives in an old barn on Edisto Island, South Carolina.

Ron Rash is the author of the 2009 PEN/Faulkner finalist and New York Times best-seller *Serena* and *Above the Waterfall*, in addition to four prizewinning novels, including *The Cove, One Foot in Eden, Saints at the River*, and *The World Made Straight*; four collections of poems; and six collections of stories, among them *Burning Bright*, which won the 2010 Frank O'Connor International Short Story Award, and *Chemistry and Other Stories*, which was a finalist for the 2007 PEN/Faulkner Award. Twice the recipient of the O. Henry Prize, he teaches at Western Carolina University.

M.O. Walsh is from Baton Rouge, Louisiana. He is the author of the story collection *The Prospect of Magic* and the novel *My Sunshine Away*, which was a *New York Times* bestseller and won the Pat Conroy Book Award for Southern Fiction. He currently teaches at the University of New Orleans where he directs the Creative Writing Workshop MFA program.

Born in Boston, Massachusetts, and a graduate of Wellesley College, **Ingrid Thoft** worked as a tech, entertainment, and education writer. Her desire to create a believable PI character led her to the certificate program in private investigation at the University of Washington. She is the author of the critically acclaimed novels *Duplicity, Identity, Loyalty*, and *Brutality*.

Jill McCorkle is the author of ten books—four story collections and six novels—five of which have been selected as *New York Times* Notable Books. The recipient of the New England Book Award, the John Dos Passos Prize for Excellence in Literature, and the North Carolina Prize for Literature, she teaches writing at North Carolina State University and lives in Hillsborough, North Carolina.

Erik Storey is a former ranch hand, wilderness guide, dogsled musher, and hunter. He spent his childhood summers growing up on his great-grandfather's homestead or in a remote cabin in Colorado's Flat Tops wilderness. He has earned a number of sharpshooter and marksman qualifications. He is the author of two Clyde Barr novels, *Nothing Short of Dying* and *A Promise to Kill*. He and his family live in Grand Junction, Colorado.

A native of Edgefield, South Carolina, **J. Drew Lanham** is the author of *The Home Place: Memoirs of a Colored Man's Love Affair with Nature*. He is a birder, naturalist, and hunter-conservationist who has published essays and poetry in publications including *Orion, Audubon, Flycatcher*, and *Wilderness*, and in several anthologies, including *The Colors of Nature, State of the Heart, Bartram's Living Legacy*, and *Carolina Writers at Home*. An Alumni Distinguished Professor of Wildlife Ecology and Master Teacher at Clemson University, he and his family live in the Upstate of South Carolina.

J. Todd Scott has been a federal agent with the DEA for more than twenty years, and is the author of *The Far Empty* and *High White Sun*. A Kentucky native, he now resides in the Southwest.

Frank Bill is the author of the novels *The Savage* and *Donnybrook* (a film directed by Tim Sutton), as well as the story collection *Crimes in Southern Indiana*, one of *GQ*'s favorite books of 2011 and a Daily Beast best debut of 2011. He lives and writes in Southern Indiana.

Eric Rickstad is the *New York Times* and *USA Today* bestselling author of the Canaan Crime Series, including *The Names of Dead Girls, The Silent Girls*, and *Lie In Wait*. His first novel *Reap* was a *New York Times* Noteworthy novel. His latest novel is *What Remains of Her*.

William Boyle is from Brooklyn, New York. He is the author of *Gravesend, Death Don't Have No Mercy, The Lonely Witness*, and *A Friend Is a Gift You Give Yourself*. He lives in Oxford, Mississippi.

Scott Gould is the author of the story collection, *Strangers to Temptation*. His work has appeared in *Kenyon Review, Crazyhorse, New Madrid Journal, Carolina Quarterly, Black Warrior Review, New Ohio Review, Bull, New Stories from the South*, and *The Bitter Southerner*, among others. He is currently chair of the creative writing department at the South Carolina Governor's School for the Arts and Humanities. And he is looking for a good deal on a bamboo 4-weight with medium action.

Mark Powell is the author of five novels, most recently *Small Treasons* from Gallery/Simon & Schuster, a Spring SIBA Okra Pick and a "Best of the Year" from *Southern Living*. He has received fellowships from the National Endowment for the Arts, the Breadloaf and Sewanee Writers' Conferences, and in 2014 was a Fulbright Fellow to Slovakia. He lives in the mountains of North Carolina and teaches at Appalachian State University.

Natalie Baszile is the author of the novel, *Queen Sugar*, which is being adapted for TV by writer/director, Ava DuVernay, and co-produced by Oprah Winfrey. *Queen Sugar* was named one of the *San Francisco Chronicles*' Best Books of 2014, was long-listed for the Crooks Corner Southern Book Prize, and nominated for an NAACP Image Award. Her nonfiction work has appeared in *The Rumpus, Buzzfeed, Lenny Letter, The Best Women's Travel Writing Volume 9, O: The Oprah Magazine,* and elsewhere. She lives in San Francisco.

Michael Farris Smith is the author of *The Fighter, Desperation Road, Rivers,* and *The Hands Of Strangers*. His novels have appeared on Best of the Year lists with *Esquire, Southern Living, Book Riot,* and numerous others, and have been named Indie Next List, Barnes & Noble Discover, and Amazon Best of the Month selections. His essays have appeared in *The New York Times, Bitter Southerner, Writer's Bone,* and more. He lives in Oxford, Mississippi, with his wife and daughters.

Chris Offutt is the author of *Country Dark, Kentucky Straight, Out of the Woods, The Same River Twice, No Heroes, The Good Brother,* and *My Father the Pornographer*. He also wrote screenplays for "True Blood," "Treme," and "Weeds." His work is in many anthologies, including *Best American Short Stories, Best American Essays,* and *The Pushcart Prize: Best of the Small Presses*. He grew up in the hills of eastern Kentucky, and currently lives in rural Lafayette County near Oxford, Mississippi.

Leigh Ann Henion is the *New York Times* bestselling author of *Phenomenal: A Hesitant Adventurer's Search for Wonder in the Natural World*. She has contributed to *The Washington Post* Magazine, *Smithsonian, Sierra, Orion, Backpacker, Oxford American, Southern Living,* and a variety of other publications. Henion is the recipient of four Lowell Thomas Awards, and her work has been cited in three editions of *The Best American Travel Writing*.

Gabino Iglesias is a writer, journalist, and book reviewer living in Austin, Texas. He's the author of *Zero Saints*, *Hungry Darkness*, and *Gutmouth*. His reviews have appeared in *Electric Literature*, *The Rumpus*, *3AM* Magazine, *Marginalia*, *The Collagist*, *Heavy Feather Review*, *Crimespree*, *Out of the Gutter*, *Vol. 1 Brooklyn*, *HorrorTalk*, *Verbicide*, and many other print and online venues.

Ray McManus is a native of South Carolina where he lives and dies every day. He is the author of four books of poetry: *Punch*, *Red Dirt Jesus*, *Driving through the Country before You Are Born*. He is also the co-editor of the anthology *Found Anew*. Ray is a professor of English at the University of South Carolina Sumter, where he teaches Irish Literature, Southern Literature, and creative writing, as well as directs the South Carolina Center for Oral Narrative.

Jim Minick is the author of five books, including *Fire Is Your Water*, a debut novel released in 2017. His memoir, *The Blueberry Years*, won the Best Nonfiction Book of the Year from the Southern Independent Booksellers Association. His work has appeared in many publications including *Poets & Writers*, *Oxford American*, *Shenandoah*, *Orion*, *San Francisco Chronicle*, *Encyclopedia of Appalachia*, *Conversations with Wendell Berry*, *Appalachian Journal*, and *The Sun*. Currently, he teaches at Augusta University and Converse College.

C.J. Box is the #1 *New York Times* bestselling author of 24 novels including the Joe Pickett series. He won the Edgar Award for Best Novel and many other awards. He was recently given the 2016 Western Heritage Award for Literature. The novels have been translated into 27 languages and they're the basis for two television series now in development. He and his wife Laurie live on their ranch in Wyoming.

Todd Davis is the author of six books of poetry, most recently, *Native Species* and *Winterkill*, both published by Michigan State University Press. His nonfiction appears in such magazines as *Gray's Sporting Journal* and *Anglers Journal*, and his poems have been published in such noted journals as *American Poetry Review*, *Alaska Quarterly Review*, *Iowa Review*, *North American Review*, *Missouri Review*, *Gettysburg Review*, *Orion*, and *Poetry Northwest*. He teaches environmental studies, creative writing, and American literature at Pennsylvania State University's Altoona College.

Rebecca Gayle Howell is the author of *American Purgatory* and *Render / An Apocalypse*. Her awards include fellowships from the Fine Arts Work Center and the Carson McCullers Center, as well as a Pushcart Prize. Howell is the James Still Writer-in-Residence at the Hindman Settlement School in Knott County, Kentucky and the poetry editor for *Oxford American*. She is the 2019 United StatesArtists Fellow.

Silas House is the author of five novels, including the *New York Times* bestseller *A Parchment of Leaves*. He is a frequent contributor to the *New York Times* and a former commentator for NPR's *All Things Considered*. House is a member of the Fellowship of Southern Writers and is the winner of the E. B. White Award, the Nautilus Award, the Appalachian Book of the Year, the Hobson Medal for Literature, and other honors. His latest novel is *Southernmost*.

PUBLISHING
New & Extraordinary
VOICES FROM THE
AMERICAN SOUTH

Founded in 1995, HUB CITY PRESS has emerged as the South's premier independent literary press. Focused on finding and spotlighting new and extraordinary voices from the American South, the press has published over eighty high-caliber literary works. Hub City is interested in books with a strong sense of place and is committed to introducing a diverse roster of lesser-heard Southern voices. We are funded by the National Endowment for the Arts, the South Carolina Arts Commission and hundreds of donors across the Carolinas.

RECENT HUB CITY PRESS TITLES

The Magnetic Girl • Jessica Handler

Let Me Out Here • Emily W. Pease

Outside Agitator: The Civil Rights Struggle of Cleveland Sellers • Adam Parker

What Luck, This Life • Kathryn Schwille

Rodeo in Reverse • Lindsey Alexander

The Wooden King • Thomas McConnell

Whiskey & Ribbons • Leesa Cross-Smith